CADETTE AND SENIOR
GIRL SCOUT HANDBOOK

Girl Scouts of the U.S.A.

830 Third Avenue

New York, N.Y. 10022

GIRL SCOUTS OF THE U.S.A.

Betty F. Pilsbury, *President*
Frances Hesselbein, *National Executive Director*

Inquiries related to the *Cadette and Senior Girl Scout Handbook* should be directed to Program, Girl Scouts of the U.S.A., 830 Third Avenue, New York, N.Y. 10022.

© 1987 by Girl Scouts of the United States of America
All rights reserved
First Impression 1987
Printed in the United States of America
ISBN 0-88441-342-X
10 9 8 7 6

Credits

Director, Program Group
Sharon Woods Hussey

Manager, Program Development
Harriet S. Mosatche, Ph.D.

Director, Graphics and Design
Michael Chanwick

Design Studio
Keithley and Associates

Cover Design
George Koizumi

Illustrator
Jeffrey Terreson

Authors/Contributors
Harriet S. Mosatche, Ph.D.
Sharon Woods Hussey
Candace White Ciraco
Verna Lewis Simpkins
Patricia Connally
Toni Eubanks
Phyllis Proctor
Maria Cecilia Cordeiro
Gayle Davis

Editor
Susan Eno

This handbook contains sections that were adapted from *You Make the Difference: The Handbook for Cadette and Senior Girl Scouts* (1980) and *From Dreams to Reality: Adventures in Careers* (1977).

CONTENTS

I.

ABOUT GIRL SCOUTING

Welcome to the expanding worlds of Cadette and Senior Girl Scouting! Whether you are a Cadette Girl Scout or a Senior Girl Scout, you are going to discover exciting new challenges. You will have ever-increasing opportunities to develop and test your leadership skills, to explore careers, to travel, to find yourself and your place in the world around you. If you have never been a Girl Scout before, you will also be introduced to the philosophy and traditions that unite Girl Scouts everywhere. You will find that you are part of a worldwide sisterhood that reaches all around the globe. Whether new to Girl Scouting or a long-time member, you are embarking on a fun-filled adventure that will enrich your life.

Using Your Handbook

This handbook will help you get the most out of your Girl Scout experience. It includes sections on how to keep fit and healthy; ways to manage your time and your money; dating, relationships with your family, and dealing with peer pressure; Leader-in-Training and Counselor-in-Training projects; forms of troop/group government; trips to Girl Scout national centers and planning for special events closer to home; service at the community and national levels; global and environmental awareness; ways to help you look ahead to the future, including possible careers you might wish to explore; and much, much more.

You may find it helpful to think of this handbook as an idea bank and reference tool. Scan the entire contents of the handbook before exploring any one chapter in depth. There is no single correct way to proceed, so if you familiarize yourself with all the possibilities, you can tailor your plans to suit your needs and interests.

Chapter 9 describes the special recognitions available to Cadette and Senior Girl Scouts. They include leadership awards, pins and patches for career exploration, Challenge pins, Service Training bars, interest projects, and the Girl Scout Silver and Gold Awards. All the information in the preceding chapters will not only provide you with activity ideas and helpful information, but will also help you complete requirements for these recognitions. If you are interested in earning recognitions, you will find it helpful to periodically review this chapter. You may find that you are already on the way to earning a recognition and you can chart a course for completing one. Or, you may be intrigued by the potential experiences in earning a particular recognition and develop a specific plan for achieving it.

GIRL SCOUT INTEREST PROJECTS

The *Cadette and Senior Girl Scout Handbook* can also be used to help you complete the many activities in *Cadette and Senior Girl Scout Interest Projects*, a companion piece to this book. Working on interest projects is one of the many ways that you can have fun, expand friendships, increase your skills, and give service to your community. For every interest project you complete, you'll earn a recognition patch that you can wear on your uniform insignia sash. Cadette Girl Scouts may also earn the badges with tan backgrounds that are described in *Girl Scout Badges and Signs*.

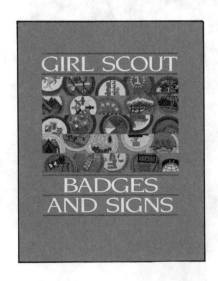

Fitting It All In

"How can I possibly do Girl Scouting and pursue my other interests too? There just isn't enough time!" Sound familiar? Many girls today have tremendous demands on their time. There is schoolwork, dating, after-school sports—just to name a few. But Girl Scouting can be a part of all of this.

To give you an example of how things you do in Girl Scouting and outside of it can blend together, try this exercise.

Write down what you do in a week. Don't get too elaborate, just make a list of the main things that happen to you Monday through Sunday. Once the list is completed, take a look at it. Did you remember ordinary things like how you get to school (riding a bus, biking, driving)? How about doing homework or planning what to wear to school or for a special date? If you find that you have some holes, fill them in.

Look at each activity and see if and how it might fulfill a requirement for a Girl Scout recognition. For instance, your regular babysitting job might count toward earning your Career Exploration pin.

The key is to find ways of making Girl Scouting a part of things that you already do. Think about which of your interests could become a part of your Girl Scout experience.

Worlds of Interest

Girl Scout activities are grouped into large subject areas called worlds of interest. There are five of these worlds.

The World of Well-Being explores physical and emotional health. The activities in this world will help you learn about exercise and nutrition, develop consumer and safety awareness, find out more about your talents and feelings, and increase your skills in interpersonal relationships.

The World of People focuses on family and friends, citizenship in the community, international friendship, and global issues. This world will help you increase your understanding and appreciation of other cultures, both here and abroad, as well as learn more about your own heritage.

The World of Today and Tomorrow will help you to become aware of ways in which you can affect the world and to gain some insights into what the future holds. In this world you'll find activities to help you discover the hows and whys of life on earth. You will also find opportunities to develop business skills and explore the many technologies that touch your daily life.

The World of the Arts includes the whole range of arts—visual, performing, and literary. Activities in this world will help you to enjoy and express yourself through various art forms and also to appreciate the artistic talents and contributions of others.

The World of the Out-of-Doors covers the many experiences possible in an outdoor setting—everything from recreation to nature and ecological studies, as well as camping in tune with today's concern for the natural environment. Activities in this world will help you understand, enjoy, and appreciate the out-of-doors.

In addition to all the activities included in the five worlds of interest, there are many activities that are related specifically to the traditions of Girl Scouting.

The Girl Scout Promise and Law

Every Girl Scout, whether girl or adult, agrees to live by the Promise and Law.

THE GIRL SCOUT PROMISE

On my honor, I will try:
To serve God and my country,
To help people at all times,
And to live by the Girl Scout Law.

This is your promise to try to live up to the teachings of your own religious faith while, at the same time, respecting the beliefs of others; to be a good citizen of your country; to help other people in small, everyday ways as well as in large ones; and to live by the following Law:

THE GIRL SCOUT LAW

I will do my best:

- to be honest
- to be fair
- to help where I am needed
- to be cheerful
- to be friendly and considerate
- to be a sister to every Girl Scout
- to respect authority
- to use resources wisely
- to protect and improve the world around me
- to show respect for myself and others through my words and actions.

Used thoughtfully and often in your everyday life, the Promise and Law can help you take action when you are faced with a decision and can help you develop the personal values that will give meaning and direction to your life.

If you have never been a Girl Scout before, you will make the Girl Scout Promise for the first time, officially, at a ceremony called an *investiture*. You will also receive your Girl Scout membership pin at that time.

The Four Program Emphases: Girl Scout Goals for Girls

The four program emphases represent the goals of Girl Scout program—the ways in which it is hoped you will grow as a result of participation in Girl Scouting.

1. Developing Self-Potential:

Developing self to achieve your full individual potential.
- Foster feelings of self-acceptance and unique self-worth.
- Promote perception of self as competent, responsible, and open to new experiences and challenges.
- Encourage personal growth.

2. Relating to Others:

Relating to others with increasing understanding, skill, and respect.
- Help develop sensitivity to others and respect for their needs, feelings, and rights.
- Promote an understanding and appreciation of individual, cultural, religious, and racial differences.
- Promote the ability to build friendships and working relationships.

3. Developing Values:

Developing values to guide your actions and to provide the foundation for sound decision-making.
- Help develop a meaningful set of values and ethics that will guide your actions.
- Foster an ability to make decisions that are consistent with your values and that reflect respect for the rights and needs of others.
- Encourage you to reexamine your ideals as you grow and change.

4. Contributing to Society:

Contributing to the improvement of society through the use of your abilities and leadership skills, working in cooperation with others.
- Develop concern for the well-being of your community and its people.
- Promote an understanding of how the quality of community life affects your own life and the whole of society.
- Encourage you to use your skills to work with others for the benefit of all.

The Girl Scout Uniform and Insignia

As a member of the Girl Scout Movement, you are entitled to wear the Girl Scouts of the U.S.A. membership pin and the World pin. These pins symbolize that you belong to Girl Scouting in the United States and are also part of an international sisterhood. The three broad parts of the trefoil-shaped membership pin represent the three parts of the Girl Scout Promise. The symbol of the World Association of Girl Guides and Girl Scouts has the same trefoil shape because Girl Guides and Girl Scouts everywhere make a three-part Promise. The World pin may be worn by all Girl Scouts and Girl Guides, along with the membership pin of their country.

You are also entitled to wear the Girl Scout uniform. The uniform is a form of identification showing that all Girl Scouts are a part of the same Movement.

Wearing your uniform at meetings, when you participate in ceremonies, when you travel as a Girl Scout, when you attend an event as part of a Girl Scout group, and when you attend church, temple, or synagogue on a special Girl Scout day is one way to show you belong.

Girl Scout insignia are the patches, pins, and special identifications you wear on your uniform. They include the recognitions you earn, such as those listed in Chapter 9, as well as insignia that all Girl Scouts wear.

Age Levels

Any girl who is five through 17 years old or in kindergarten through twelfth grade can become a Girl Scout in the United States. Girls of every race, culture, and religion are included. The following chart illustrates some of the key elements of each of the five age levels in Girl Scouting.

Girl Scouting at the Five Age Levels

	Age or Grade	Form of Troop Government	Recognitions
DAISY	5–6 years old or in kindergarten or first grade	Daisy Girl Scout Circle	Certificate when Daisy Girl Scout year is begun and completed
BROWNIE	6–8 years old or in first, second, or third grade	Brownie Girl Scout Ring with committee	Brownie Girl Scout Try-Its Bridge to Junior Girl Scouts patch Dabbler badge
JUNIOR	8–11 years old or in third, fourth, fifth, or sixth grade	Patrol system, executive board, or town meeting	Badges Signs (Rainbow, Sun, Satellite, World) Junior Aide patch Bridge to Cadette Girl Scouts patch
CADETTE	11–14 years old or in sixth, seventh, eighth, or ninth grade	Patrol system, executive board, or town meeting	Tan badges Interest project patches From Dreams to Reality patch Cadette Girl Scout Leadership Award Leader-in Training and Counselor-in-Training Project pins Cadette Girl Scout Challenge Service Training bars Religious recognitions Girl Scout Silver Award Bridge to Senior Girl Scouts patch
SENIOR	14–17 years old or in ninth, tenth, eleventh, or twelfth grade	Patrol system, executive board, or town meeting	Interest project patches Career Exploration pin Senior Girl Scout Leadership Award Senior Girl Scout Challenge Leader-in-Training and Counselor-in-Training Project pins Service Training bars Religious recognitions Ten-Year Award Girl Scout Gold Award Bridge to Adult Girl Scouts pin

There will probably be many times when you, as a Cadette or Senior Girl Scout, will be helping younger girls with their Girl Scout activities.

Adults in Girl Scouting

There are many adults in many different positions who help make Girl Scouting possible. Most important is the Girl Scout leader or adviser—a volunteer who has taken special training for her job as a partner to the girls with whom she works.

Leaders help in planning, share expertise, and find other resource people who can also help with various parts of Girl Scout program. In some troops, the leader may have one or more assistants. In recognition of the vital role that Girl Scout leaders and assistant leaders fill in Girl Scouting, Leader's Day—April 22—is set aside each year to honor them.

Many other adults also help to make Girl Scouting possible in the area where you live. Along with leaders and the other adults who work with girls directly, these people are all part of your Girl Scout council.

A *Girl Scout council* is a group of women and men who are responsible for administering Girl Scouting in a specific area. It is administered by volunteers who employ a professional staff to help carry out the work. Their work includes a wide variety of activities, such as starting new troops and finding meeting places for them, training leaders, operating camps, recruiting members from all segments of the community, and raising money for Girl Scouting. There are more than 300 Girl Scout councils across the country, all chartered by Girl Scouts of the United States of America (GSUSA).

GSUSA directs and coordinates the Girl Scout Movement in the United States. It does this through the activities of the National Board of Directors, the National Board committees, and the national staff. Every three years, Girl Scout councils elect delegates to the National Council of Girl Scouts of the U.S.A. This body elects the members of the National Board of Directors and officers and determines general policy for matters affecting all Girl Scouts throughout the United States.

Membership dues from everyone in the Girl Scout Movement in the United States are paid to the national organization, GSUSA. GSUSA uses this money to provide many services to all its members in this country and to USA Girl Scouts Overseas. For example, it publishes books like this handbook, operates the national centers (see below), and secures grants for special opportunities and events. GSUSA also coordinates national and international events (wider opportunities) for Cadette and Senior Girl Scouts, and prepares a publication called *Wider Ops: Girl Scout Wider Opportunities* describing these events.

Juliette Gordon Low Girl Scout National Center

GIRL SCOUT NATIONAL CENTERS

There are two Girl Scout national centers that are owned and operated by Girl Scouts of the U.S.A. Girl Scouts from all across the country come to these centers to participate in activities as different as the settings of the centers themselves.

Juliette Gordon Low Girl Scout National Center, located in the heart of Savannah, Georgia, is the birthplace of the founder of Girl Scouting in the United States (see pages 15–18). More than 400 troops a year travel to this Registered National Historic Landmark, now restored to its original graciousness and furnished in 1870s style. Here you can learn more about Juliette Low, her family, and her work with Girl Scouts, and discover for yourself what an extraordinary woman Juliette Low was.

Edith Macy Conference Center

Edith Macy Conference Center is a year-round educational facility for Girl Scout adults that also offers some events for girls who are ages 13–18. This center is situated 35 miles north of New York City, on a 269-acre site in Briarcliff Manor, New York. Adults in Girl Scouting may also come to the John J. Creedon Center on the property of Edith Macy Conference Center. Here, participants learn more about camping and outdoor activities for Girl Scouts. Camp Andree Clark, GSUSA's camp adjacent to the conference center, covers an area of almost 200 acres of wooded hills, and includes facilities for traveling troops.

More information about the Girl Scout national centers is included in *Wider Ops: Girl Scout Wider Opportunities*.

John J. Creedon Center

Antigua and Barbuda*
Argentina
Australia
Austria
Bahamas
Bahrain
Bangladesh
Barbados
Belgium
Belize*
Benin*
Bolivia
Botswana
Brazil
Brunei Darussalam*
Burkina Faso*
   (formerly Upper Volta)
Burundi*
Cameroon*
Canada
Central African Republic*
Chile
China, Republic of
Colombia
Costa Rica
Cyprus
Czechoslovakia*
Denmark
Dominica*
Dominican Republic
Ecuador
Egypt
El Salvador
Fiji*
Finland
France
Gambia, The
Germany
Ghana
Greece

Grenada*
Guatemala
Guyana
Haiti
Honduras*
Hong Kong
Iceland
India
Indonesia
Ireland
Israel
Italy
Ivory Coast*
Jamaica
Japan
Jordan
Kenya
Kiribati*
Korea
Kuwait
Lebanon
Lesotho
Liberia
Libya
Liechtenstein
Luxembourg
Madagascar
Malaysia
Malta
Mauritius
Mexico
Monaco
Nepal
Netherlands
Netherlands Antilles
New Zealand
Nicaragua*
Nigeria
Norway
Oman*
Pakistan

Panama
Papua New Guinea*
Paraguay
Peru
Philippines
Portugal
Rwanda*
St. Lucia*
St. Vincent and
   the Grenadines
Senegal*
Sierra Leone
Singapore
Solomon Islands*
South Africa
Spain
Sri Lanka
Sudan
Suriname*
Swaziland*
Sweden
Switzerland
Tanzania
Thailand
Togo*
Tonga*
Trinidad and Tobago
Turkey
Tuvalu*
Uganda
United Arab Emirates
United Kingdom
United States of America
Uruguay*
Vanuatu*
Venezuela
(North) Yemen*
Zambia
Zimbabwe

*Starred names are associate members

The World Association of Girl Guides and Girl Scouts

Girl Scouts of the U.S.A. is a member of the World Association of Girl Guides and Girl Scouts (WAGGGS), which is why you are entitled to wear a World pin. The worldwide Movement has Girl Guide or Girl Scout associations in over 100 countries. All of these associations are united by common ideals, as expressed in the Girl Scout Promise (see page 4). The wording is different in different countries, but the meaning is the same.

The World Association was chartered in 1928, during an international conference attended by adult representatives of Girl Guide and Girl Scout associations from all around the world. The original membership of WAGGGS included associations in 27 countries. The growth of the Girl Guide/Girl Scout Movement in those early days was truly remarkable, especially in view of the world conditions that prevailed. For example, rapid transportation and many of the techniques of communication that we enjoy today did not exist.

Today, the Movement continues to grow, especially among the emerging nations of the world. Every three years, representatives of every Girl Guide or Girl Scout organization in the world meet at a World Conference to share ideas and make decisions that are important to Girl Guides and Girl Scouts everywhere. Every time a World Conference is held, new members are admitted. Of the countries represented in the World Association of Girl Guides and Girl Scouts today, more than half have joined since 1960. The list of members as of the 1990 World Conference appears on the opposite page.

THE WORLD CENTERS

As part of its ongoing effort to promote international friendship, the World Association of Girl Guides and Girl Scouts operates four world centers: Our Chalet, located high on a mountain near Adelboden, Switzerland; Our Cabaña, near Cuernavaca, Mexico; Sangam, in Pune, India; and Pax Lodge, in London, England. Pax Lodge, named to honor the efforts of Lord and Lady Baden-

Our Chalet

Our Cabaña

Sangam

Pax Lodge

Powell, is a residential center of international Girl Guide/Girl Scout gatherings. For more information about the centers, write to: Program Group, Girl Scouts of the U.S.A., 830 Third Avenue, New York, N.Y. 10022.

Girl Scout/Girl Guide Traditions

There are many symbols and customs that are shared by all Girl Scouts and Girl Guides. One is the *Girl Scout sign,* a form of greeting exchanged whenever Girl Scouts or Girl Guides meet. Three fingers on the right hand are extended to symbolize the three parts of the Promise.

The *Girl Scout handshake* is another form of greeting used by Girl Scouts and Girl Guides all around the world. It is done by shaking hands with the left hand while making the Girl Scout sign with the right. The left hand is the one nearest the heart and therefore signifies friendship.

The *quiet sign* is used in meetings and other gatherings to quiet the group. The sign is made by raising your right hand high. As people in the group see the quiet sign, they stop talking and also raise their right hands. In a matter of moments, the whole group is silent.

Sometimes, in a meeting or at a campsite, Girl Scouts and Girl Guides form a *friendship circle*. Everyone stands in a circle and each person crosses her right arm over her left, clasping hands with her friends on both sides. Everyone is silent as a *friendship squeeze* is passed from hand to hand. The friendship circle stands for an unbroken chain of friendship with Girl Scouts and Girl Guides all around the world.

Girl Scouts and Girl Guides everywhere have the same *slogan*, "Do a good turn daily," and the same *motto*, "Be prepared." The slogan is a reminder of the many ways, both large and small, that each of us can contribute to the lives of others. A Girl Scout service project (see pages 115–119) is a type of good turn that takes planning and time. The motto reminds us that we must be not only *willing*, but *able* to give service.

A special day is observed in every Girl Scout and Girl Guide country: February 22, known as *Thinking Day*. This is the birthday of both Robert, Lord Baden-Powell, who founded the Boy Scout movement in England; and his wife, Olave, Lady Baden-Powell. Olave continued the work of Agnes Baden-Powell, who started Girl Guiding, the Scouting movement for girls. Olave served as World Chief Guide until her death in 1977. Juliette Gordon Low brought the ideals of this movement to the U.S.A., where she founded Girl Scouting in 1912.

Girl Guides and Girl Scouts make a special effort to meet on Thinking Day, to exchange greetings with their sisters in other countries, and to give contributions to the Thinking Day Fund. This Fund is used to promote the Girl Guide/Girl Scout Movement throughout the world and to help Girl Guide and Girl Scout organizations in various countries, especially during the years when these organizations are being formed and getting under way. The Thinking Day Fund has provided bicycles for trainers and leaders to reach girls in outlying areas, training in child care, nutrition, and hygiene, and many other services and resources that are needed.

Ceremonies

Ceremonies play an important part in Girl Scouting. They are used to help you celebrate special occasions, such as the welcoming of new members to your troop, the presentation of awards, or the Girl Scout birthday. They can be used to open or close a meeting. They can be short or long, formal or informal. They may include girls in your troop or group, other girls in Girl Scouting, Girl Scout leaders or other adults, and special guests like parents, relatives, and friends. They can be held by large groups or small groups, outdoors or indoors, and can include anything you choose.

Below are some ceremonies that are especially important in Girl Scouting:

- An *investiture ceremony* is held to welcome someone into Girl Scouting for the first time.
- A *bridging ceremony* is held when you "cross the bridge" to the next level in Girl Scouting.
- A *rededication ceremony* is held at special times when Girl Scouts want to renew their Girl Scout Promise and review what the Girl Scout Law means to them. Troops usually hold one at the beginning and end of each troop year. A Girl Scout member can take part in many rededication ceremonies.
- A *Court of Awards* ceremony is one at which girls receive recognitions they have earned.
- A *Girl Scouts' Own* is a special ceremony created by a troop or group around a theme.

The following types of ceremonies—candlelight ceremonies and flag ceremonies—are often used as part of larger ceremonies, but they can also take place on their own.

Candlelight Ceremonies

Candlelight ceremonies help girls to think about the meaning of their Girl Scout Promise and Law. Three large candles are used to represent the three parts of the Promise, and ten smaller candles represent the ten parts of the Law.

Flag Ceremonies

A flag ceremony honors the American flag as the symbol of our country. As part of a flag ceremony, you say the Pledge of Allegiance. You might also sing "The Star-Spangled Banner" or some other song honoring our country, such as "God Bless America" or "America, the Beautiful." For information on how to conduct a flag ceremony, see *Outdoor Education in Girl Scouting*.

PLANNING A CEREMONY

No matter what kind of ceremony you are having, good planning is essential so that the ceremony will be really meaningful. Basically, any ceremony has three parts—the opening, the main part, and the closing.

The *opening* part of the ceremony can be used to welcome guests, tell the purpose of the ceremony, and set the mood for the occasion. For example, it might be quiet, festive, or serious.

The *main*, or *central* part of the ceremony focuses on the reason you have gathered people together. It might include such things as poems, songs, choral readings, dramatics, or candle lighting.

The *closing* part of the ceremony may summarize the ceremony. It might include forming a friendship circle, saying good-byes or thank-yous to special guests, or singing a closing song.

For more information regarding the types of ceremonies and relevant procedures, refer to *Ceremonies in Girl Scouting*.

Juliette Low and Girl Scouting in the U.S.A.

Girl Scouting in the United States was founded by a most remarkable woman named Juliette Gordon Low. Back in the late 1800s, before most of today's great-grandmothers were even born, Juliette Low was something of a revolutionary—not the kind who destroys, but the kind who creates. She was an environmentalist, a crusader, a woman dedicated to the service of others. Above all, she was certain that the future belonged to the young and that they had better start right now to do something worthwhile about it.

Juliette was born into the wealthy Gordon family of Savannah, Georgia, on Halloween—October 31, 1860—a few months before the start of the American Civil War. Known to her family and friends as Daisy, she was a person of many talents, many interests, and a very strong sense of determination. She refused to let adversity stand in her way. Her hearing problems that eventually developed into almost total deafness never stopped her from pursuing her goals.

Juliette married an Englishman named William Low and went to live in England and Scotland. However, the marriage was not a happy one and Juliette was in the process of getting a divorce when her husband died. After that, she traveled

Juliette Gordon and William Low on their wedding day

for several years and then settled in Paris with the idea of studying sculpture. However, she was soon to meet a man who started her on a venture that would become her life's work. That man was Sir Robert (later Lord) Baden-Powell, an English general and war hero who had founded the Boy Scout movement only three years earlier.

Lord and Lady Baden-Powell with their good friend, Juliette Low

The Boy Scout movement had caught on instantly and had already spread to several other countries. In England it had also resulted in the formation of a similar organization for girls. It was the girls themselves who took the initiative, forming into groups similar to those their brothers had joined. There was so much interest among these girls that Baden-Powell asked his sister, Agnes, to give them an organization of their own. So Agnes officially established an association of Girl Guides in 1910. By the time another year rolled by, there were Girl Guides or Scouts in Australia, South Africa, and Finland. In the next year, similar groups were formed in Sweden, Denmark, Poland, and Canada.

This new movement was just the sort of thing that appealed to Juliette Low, and soon she was back in Scotland, leading a Guide group of her own. As her interest in the Girl Guides grew, Juliette was eager to introduce the program to American girls. Not one to waste time, she was soon on her way to the United States. There she telephoned an old friend to say, "Come right over. I've got something for the girls of Savannah, and all America, and all the world, and we're going to start it tonight."

The time was 1912. Women led far more restricted lives than they do now, but change was in the air. Women were beginning to realize that many activities were barred to them through custom and prejudice alone. They were becoming convinced of their ability to do hundreds of things which up until then only "radicals" and "eccentrics" had even suggested women might do. It was exactly the right time to launch a program that was designed to have girls look beyond their sheltered lives and show them the possibilities for pleasure and adventure in the great outdoors. Most important, Girl Scouting was to point the way to independence through experiences that were fun while they broadened individual knowledge and skills.

The first meeting of Girl Scouts was in Savannah on March 12, 1912. In no time, troops were forming elsewhere. By the time of World War I, there were enough Girl Scouts in the United States to make a real contribution to the war effort. These girls helped to realize Juliette Low's dream of girls' learning to be active, vital citizens of their country.

Juliette Low and her girls in front of Daisy's own flag

The first Girl Scouts used the English Girl Guide handbook and later an adaptation written by an American naturalist, Walter John Hoxie. In many ways, that American version foreshadowed the thinking of American women today. While it emphasized proper preparation for "housewifery," it also advised girls that "really well-educated women can make a good income" as architects, doctors, accountants, scientists, and aviators. Although the wording was different, the handbook also reflected such present-day concerns as ecology, organic foods, organic cosmetics, physical fitness, and pollution control. The 1916 version of this handbook, written by Juliette Low herself, made provision for an aviation badge—this at a time when aviation was in its infancy! Juliette already saw a role for women in this exciting new field.

Juliette Low believed that girls could and should plan their own program, make their own decisions, run their own troop. She saw their adult leaders as helpers and advisers, never as "directors." Whenever a new program idea was suggested and some adult committee member questioned whether it would work, her answer was, "Ask the girls. If they don't like it, the Angel Gabriel himself couldn't make them accept it!" She not only loved girls, she respected them. She respected their judgments, their preferences.

Juliette Low died on January 18, 1927. A few months later, the Juliette Low World Friendship Fund was started to honor her and her vision of worldwide friendship. Every year, Girl Scouts throughout the United States give money to this fund—usually on her birthday, October 31, or on Thinking Day, February 22. Part of the money is used to send Girl Scouts to other countries and to bring

Girl Guides and Girl Scouts from other countries to the United States, while the other part goes to the Thinking Day Fund set up by the World Association of Girl Guides and Girl Scouts (see pages 10–12).

Girl Scouts in the United States also honor Juliette Low in other ways. Each year, on October 31, Girl Scout troops celebrate her birthday with a variety of ceremonies and projects. On March 12, the anniversary of the day when Juliette formed the first troop of Girl Scouts in this country, Girl Scouts celebrate the *Girl Scout birthday*. The week in which March 12 falls is designated as *Girl Scout Week*.

Juliette has also been highly honored by the United States government. During World War II, the government named a liberty ship after her. In 1948 a Juliette Gordon Low U.S. commemorative postage stamp was printed, and in 1973, her portrait was presented to the National Gallery in Washington, D.C. In 1974 Juliette was also honored by her own state of Georgia, when a bust of her was placed in the Georgia State Capitol Hall of Fame. In 1983, Congress designated that a new government office building in Savannah, Georgia, be named after the founder of Girl Scouting. It is called the Juliette Gordon Low Federal Complex.

Juliette Low is remembered as a woman who worked for peace and goodwill. Her dream was to have young people make the world a friendly, peaceful place. She wanted young people to understand themselves and others. She wanted to give something special to the world, and that was Girl Scouting. In the final paragraph of her will, she wrote, ". . . I leave and bequeath to my family my friendships, especially my beloved Girl Scouts." She never had any children of her own, but her "adopted family" of Girl Scouts numbered 167,925 at the time of her death. Today this "family" has grown to more than three million members, and every one of them owes a debt of gratitude to the woman who made it all possible—Juliette Gordon Low.

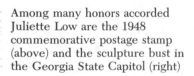

Among many honors accorded Juliette Low are the 1948 commemorative postage stamp (above) and the sculpture bust in the Georgia State Capitol (right)

2

PERSONAL DEVELOPMENT

You are in an exciting time of life, a time of discovery about yourself and your world and all who share it with you. With each day you grow toward greater self-reliance. You are becoming a more capable person on many levels. Your self-understanding is growing as you recognize strengths, talents, and abilities as well as weaknesses and areas to improve. This chapter asks you to look at yourself and others. It will explore some of the factors that contribute to your development, the way you and your peers think about yourselves, and the many relationships that are a part of your life.

The Person I Am

Talented, exhilarated, joyful, doubtful, in turmoil, smart, curious, satisfied, unhappy, anxious, proud, fearful, in love, bored, sad, moody, creative, indignant, respected, silly, adventuresome, reckless, sensitive, self-assured, confused, shy. Would you use any of these words to describe yourself at this time of your life?

You probably can think of times when two opposite terms could describe you at the same time, and you might use totally different sets of words to describe yourself on different days. You are a unique individual with your own special combination of capabilities.

TAKE A LOOK AT YOURSELF

Write down ten words that you would use to describe yourself. Think about why you selected each one and ask yourself some questions. Are there more positives, or more negatives? Would most other people agree with your list? How would your list be different from one made up a year ago? a week ago? two years from now?

You can use this simple exercise to look more closely at yourself. Try these variations. Put your list aside for a short period of time (a week or a month), then do a new one. Compare the two. Ask a family member or friend to do a list. Compare that list with your own.

___ "NOW I AM"

You will mature and develop throughout your life. As you mature physically and intellectually, you are not the same person that you were last summer or last week (or perhaps just yesterday). Think about the ways you have matured and fill in the following chart:

Example:

Once I   was a total slob _____.

Now I   am sometimes neat _____.

Once I   _____
_____.

Now I   _____
_____.

Once I   _____
_____.

Now I   _____
_____.

Once I   _____
_____.

Now I   _____
_____.

Once I   _____
_____.

Now I   _____

___ THE "ME" INTERVIEW

Many times other people recognize your strengths better than you do. For this activity you will find out what strengths people recognize in you.

Use a plain sheet of standard size paper for your interview. Title it "My Strengths." Divide it into three equal columns. Then divide the paper in half by drawing a horizontal line through the middle. This will give you six equal boxes. Label each box as shown in the illustration.

Me	Family Member	Neighbor
Male Friend	Female Friend	Teacher

Write in the "Me" box three of your strengths. Now interview five people who fit in the categories of the remaining boxes. Ask each one to name three strengths that you have. Write their responses in the appropriate boxes. At your next troop or group meeting, or with a friend or relative, discuss these questions:

1. How do you feel about what people like about you?
2. Did anybody identify a strength you didn't know you had?
3. Is there a strength you recognize in yourself that nobody else recognized? If so, how can you make people aware of it?
4. Did more than one person identify the same or similar strengths?
5. Do you remember to tell these other people what you like about them?

SELF-ESTEEM

Self-esteem, the way you perceive and judge yourself, is influenced by many things—the people who are important to you (family, friends, teachers, Girl Scout leaders), the experiences you have had, your successes and failures, and your own personality. As your life changes, so can your self-esteem.

There is a noticeable difference between people with high self-esteem and those with low self-esteem. Those with high self-esteem have faith in their abilities and are willing to make their own decisions. They are more likely to try new things, and expect to be successful. A person with high self-esteem has an advantage in life. She takes responsibility for creating her own success and happiness.

People with low self-esteem have a low opinion of themselves. They have little faith in their abilities, feel unacceptable and fearful of new situations and people. Often they need a great deal of approval, are conforming in their behavior, and are dependent on others for their well-being.

Each of us has unique qualities and abilities, for no two individuals are exactly alike. When we feel good about ourselves, we encourage others to feel good about us.

Positive Thinking

Think of at least six good things about yourself. They could be positive beliefs about your personality, appearance, talents, accomplishments, or interests. Write them down.

Now, try to think about these positive statements several times during the day. You might write them on separate index cards and scatter them in different places: in your purse, in a drawer, on the inside of your locker door, anywhere you will be sure to see them several times during the day. This exercise is not a form of bragging or being conceited about yourself. It merely helps you acknowledge your strengths and build your self-confidence. You can take the exercise one step further and write a positive statement about one of your family members, or a friend, and give it to the person.

Feelings

Feelings are a part of every experience you have:

- the excitement of your first school dance
- the sadness when thinking about someone close to you who has died
- the pride at receiving the Girl Scout Silver Award
- the disappointment of not being invited to a classmate's party
- the happiness of being selected for the math team
- the anger at being blamed for something you didn't do
- the anxiety that accompanied your first trip alone on an airplane
- the relief when you found the notebook you had thought was lost

Feelings can change from one day to the next, sometimes from one minute to the next. They affect the way you think about yourself, the way you sound, and the way you react to others. Feelings are often expressed in "body language"— your posture, your facial expressions, your gestures. You may think that your feelings don't show, but your voice or your hands or your eyes may give them away. It often helps you and the people you deal with to express your feelings openly and honestly. And of course, it's important for you to be sensitive to the feelings expressed by those around you. For instance, your mother's voice (but not her words) on the telephone tells you that something's bothering her, or your best friend is not her usual bouncy, vivacious self this morning.

HANDLING YOUR FEARS

Some feelings are more difficult to deal with than others. Fear is one of those—a common human emotion that often clouds our thinking and causes us to feel isolated. Fear takes many forms: "fear of nuclear war," "fear of heights," "fear of bringing your report card home," "fear of becoming seriously ill," "fear of delivering an oral report in school." The fact is that you are not alone in your fears. Many others share the same or similar fears. Try this activity with a group of friends to help reduce your fears.

1. Each person should think about something she is afraid of or worried about, but doesn't usually talk about.
2. She should then write down the fear on a piece of paper, fold it, and put it in a paper bag (no name should be put down).
3. After the bag is shaken, each person will take a turn reading a problem out loud and starting a discussion about it.

Nobody else will know who the fear belongs to, even if someone pulls her own. Each of you will learn that it is often very helpful to talk your fears over with someone else.

Values

At this time in your life, you are facing many challenges. You are continuing your education, preparing yourself for roles in the work world, developing relationships with peers and family, and dealing with your evolving sexuality. Through all this, your values serve as foundations for your decisions and actions.

Values are what you believe in and what are important to you in your life. Values are shaped and infuenced by your family, friends, school, religion, media, the country in which you live, your Girl Scout experience, and many other things. The more you are aware of your own values, the more your behavior will be consistent with what you truly feel and believe.

As your experiences widen, your values may change. Sometimes it can be difficult to know what your values really are—you may feel confused. Some of the issues that you may be developing values about are politics, work, relationships, health, appearance, money, recreation, and authority. This section will help you discover more about your values.

To help you explore your attitudes, values, and interests further, complete these sentences. Look for patterns in your responses:

During my free time, I like to _____

_____.

When I'm 25 years old _____

_____.

Some of the things I like best about life are _____

_____.

I could help make the world a better place by _____

_____.

Some of my weaknesses are _____

_____.

Some of my strengths are _____

_____.

I feel sad when _____

_____.

I get angry when _____

_____.

I'm happiest when _____

_____.

My friends are _____

_____.

My family is _____

_____.

WHAT ARE YOUR VALUES?

Make a list of things or ideas that are of value to you. Your list might include family, knowledge, friends, religion, happiness, freedom, health, success, fame, and many other values. Then look at your list and pick the three most important to you. What have you learned about yourself by doing this exercise? Try it again several months later and see if there are any changes.

ACT UPON YOUR VALUES

Spend at least one week cultivating and appreciating some of the things you put on your values list. If you wrote that you value your family, spend time with them and let them know how you value them. If health was on your list, take time to learn more about your health and to practice good health habits (see pages 61–65). Do this with as many topics from your list as you wish.

Make a Deal ... With Yourself

There are many ways to act upon your values. One way is to make a plan, an agreement, or a "deal" with yourself. For instance, let's say you value an attractive appearance, but you're not really happy about the way you look. Make a deal with yourself! Decide what you can do to look better (see "Making Decisions" section on pages 74–75), make a plan with manageable steps, and then do it! Also refer to other sections of the "Life Skills" chapter for concrete ideas on how to reach your goals.

CONFLICTS

Often conflicts arise that test our values. What would you do if you were in Ellen's, Marsha's, or Nicki's predicament?

Ellen knew she should have finished those math problems last night. Now she only has ten minutes before algebra class and her major homework assignment is incomplete. Bill is willing to let her copy his answers. This assignment is important and will count toward her final grade. She really wants to get a good grade, but she's always prided herself on accomplishing things on her own. What values are at stake? Does Ellen have options that won't compromise her values?

Marsha values her friendships. Being liked and accepted by her peers is very important to her. Max, whom she does not know very well, has asked her out for a date. Marsha's best friend, Kim, invites Marsha and Max to go to a concert on that evening. Kim has been going out with her boyfriend, Doug, for two years.
The day comes and the four of them go to the concert in the car Doug borrowed from his parents. The concert is great and they have a wonderful time. As Doug is driving them home, he decides to stop at a scenic lake nearby. Marsha is getting nervous because Kim and Doug have started making out in the front seat and Max is looking at her as if he wants to do the same! She likes Max, but she's not sure this is what she wants. What should Marsha do? What values does she need to consider?

Nicki is very athletic and highly values her health. She's on numerous sports teams at school and has won several athletic awards. Her best friend Susan is also an athlete. They do many things together and have a lot of the same friends. One afternoon Nicki goes over to Susan's house and finds Susan "doing" cocaine in her bedroom. Nicki is shocked, especially since Susan is an athlete and her best

friend. Susan tells Nicki that it is no big deal and that the drug is great and makes her feel fantastic. Susan then tries to talk Nicki into trying it, telling her it won't hurt her. Meanwhile, Nicki is remembering all the terrible effects of cocaine, that people have died after using it, that it's against the law, and that it's addictive. While Nicki is curious, she decides she will never try it. But, what is she going to do about her best friend? What would you do if you were Nicki? What values does she have to consider?

You may face similar conflicts in your life that test your values. When these times come, let your values guide you and you'll have less of a chance of making a mistake or doing something you'll regret later.

PROS AND CONS

As you know already, people have different values. For every value *for* (pro) something, there may be someone who has a value *against* (con) it. In order to form your own decisions and values about life, it helps to have as much

factual knowledge as possible. Knowledge gives you a foundation upon which to base your decisions. Learn about the pros and cons of values by looking at both sides of the statements made below. What could be the arguments in support of each statement? What could be the arguments against each statement? You could do this individually or get a group of people together to take different positions on each statement. Statements:

- The law should make it harder for couples with children to get a divorce.
- People should be allowed to do whatever they want as long as their actions do not harm anyone else.
- Nuclear arms should be banned worldwide.
- People should be allowed to wear whatever they want in a work setting.
- Students should be permitted to choose all their own classes.

Make up your own value statements, and see if you can develop pro and con arguments for them.

Interests

Your values may influence your interests and vice versa. What are your interests? What things do you like to do? What topics interest you? Once you've realized what your interests are, a rewarding part of your life is to explore and develop them.

Look through the book *Cadette and Senior Girl Scout Interest Projects* and make a list of those projects that interest you. After you have finished, analyze your list. Do you see a pattern in your areas of interest? Are you interested in many different topics or do your interests lead you to a few topics? You may want to choose some of the interest projects and earn recognition patches. Doing this is an excellent way to explore your interests. See the "Life Skills" chapter of this handbook for more on developing interests.

3

RELATIONSHIPS

Do you enjoy meeting new people? talking to friends? spending time with your family? sharing news with classmates? Relationships are an essential aspect of being human. They can add excitement, love, and a sense of security to your life. But they can also mean frustration, disappointment, and jealousy.

This chapter deals with some important relationships and discusses key issues that may be on your mind now—like peer pressure and dating.

Family

While relationships with people outside the family are growing in importance, the family continues to be a very important part of adolescent life. Your family can be your foundation in life—the people who give you support, who help you grow, and who love you. You do the same for them. In today's world, families come in all sizes and combinations of people and relationships. A family could be two people or thirteen people.

Families have their ups and downs, their good points and bad points. Your feelings about your family or particular family members may change as you reach adolescence. Some adolescents feel that they relate better to people in their families than to their friends. Others don't feel as close to their families as they had at one time. Some may be embarrassed by their families in certain situations or they feel that their families don't have time for them. These are all natural feelings. You'll probably find that, as with all relationships, your feelings and the dynamics in your family will change again and again throughout life.

Try some of the activities below to explore family life.

FAMILY SYMBOL

Take a few minutes to think about your family. Think of its spirit, what makes it unique. Then, think of a symbol for your family. It could be anything—a design, an animal, a person, a plant, an object—whatever. The important thing is that you feel it has meaning with regard to your family. Try doing this activity with other family members. Explain why you each chose the symbol you did.

FAMILY TIMELINE

Do some family research and make a family timeline. Record births, marriages, moves, and other important events that influenced your family. Share the timeline with your family.

WHERE IN THE WORLD IS YOUR FAMILY FROM?

Get a world map and some map pins or markers, Mark as many places as you can in the world that show where your family is from and where they are now. Ask as many family members as you can to give you their information. Show the map at a family gathering.

PICTURES WORTH THOUSANDS OF WORDS

If your family saves photographs, spend time looking through them. Get to know about the people and places in the photos.

GETTING TO KNOW YOU

Many times, we don't take the time to really get to know people—even when they're in our own family. Pick someone in your family whom you would like to know better. Plan an activity with that person that will help you to learn more about her or him.

ROLE-PLAYING

Think of some family situations and act them out with others. Experiment by taking different roles.

Some could be:

- An older sister is watching a TV program and her younger sister changes the station without asking.
- A younger sister is jealous and resentful because she feels that her older sister gets more attention, better things, and more freedom.
- Parents don't seem interested in the person whom their adolescent daughter is dating.
- After her parents' divorce, a teenage girl and her mother move in with the mother's parents.
- A parent makes too many rules for an adolescent daughter about her after-school activities.
- Two stepsisters have to share a room after their parents get married to each other and move in together.
- A younger sister wants to tag along with her older sister.
- An adolescent sister feels her adolescent brother gets more freedom and respect from their family.
- A younger brother is very upset when he finds out that his parents are getting divorced. His older sister talks with him.

OTHER FAMILIES

Spend time with families other than your own. Ask your friends to cooperate. Interview some people in other families; find out about how they celebrate, what rules they have, how they organize their lives, how they spend time together, and so forth.

YOUR FAMILY—FOR THE FUTURE

Leave a family journal so that future generations can learn about families today. Write down interesting things about your family and its life in our times. Tell the future generations what makes your family special. Keep the journal in a safe place and add to it as different family events happen.

Friendship

Friendship makes life more worthwhile, enriching, and fun. Some people seem to have a gift for making new friends, while others are often lonely, not knowing how to reach out to others. Meeting new people often creates anxiety. What will he think of me? Will she reject me if I say hello? Sometimes if a girl doesn't think very highly of herself, she expects that other people will not want to get to know her.

The ability to make friends is a valuable skill to have throughout a lifetime. Here's what Georgia did to make friends when she moved to a new school district:

Georgia's family had just moved to Newtown and she had started ninth grade two weeks ago. It seemed as if people already knew each other well and were involved in their own social activities. Georgia felt lonely and left out. She missed having people she could talk with, do things with, eat with.

On Monday morning Georgia decided that today she was going to make at least *one* friend. She thought carefully about the people in her classes she had met or had seen so far who might become her friends. She decided on Daphne, Ivan, and Cindy. Her plan was to introduce herself to each one and try to start up a conversation. She would approach one person, Daphne, today and the other two later in the week.

When Georgia arrived at school, she casually introduced herself to Daphne. Georgia told Daphne that she had recently moved to town. The two girls hit it off well and they decided to have lunch together the next day.

Making friends is not always as easy as Georgia found it. However, she did some important things that helped make the process work. Georgia had the desire to make friends. She thought carefully about which people she might get along well with. She pleasantly introduced herself, started a conversation, and followed it through with a suggestion that she and Daphne do something together.

How can you learn how to meet new people? Watch others who are successful. What do they do? Watch how they move, start a conversation, keep a conversation going, maintain eye contact.

What else can you do to make it easier to meet people? Think about the way you look. If you feel good about your appearance, you will feel more comfortable meeting people. And if you expect to make a good impression on others, you probably will. Wear clothes that you really like—one terrific outfit may be better than ten that just look okay. Experiment with your hair style. Get into better shape. See pages 61–65 on health and fitness for tips on looking and feeling your best. You might like to work on the Fashion Design and Clothing and Fashion/Fitness/Makeup interest projects.

FRIENDLY NETWORKS

Often you make new friends through friends you already have. For example, in the friend network chart shown here, Pat met Mariko first. Through Mariko, she became friends with David and Kim. Through Kim, she met Daryl, and so on. Your friends can widen your world and you can do the same for them.

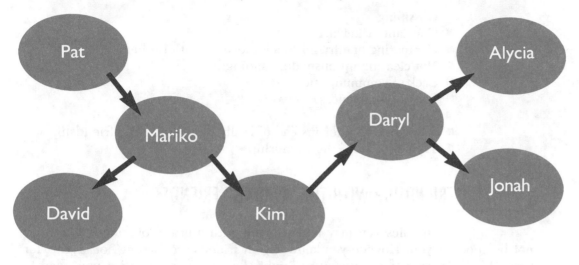

Think about the friends you have and how you met them. Make a friend network chart of your own. Think of one friend and put that person in the center circle. Then, branching off from that person, draw connecting circles of friends you met through that person.

FRIENDSHIP BENEFITS

Think of the people with whom you are friends. Why are you friends with them? to laugh with? to share confidences? to go skating with? to help you with your homework sometimes? You will probably have different reasons for different people, but all of your friendships are probably beneficial to you in one way or another. They should also be beneficial to your friends.

Think of one of your friendships. Make a list of the benefits you receive from the friendship. Alongside that list, make a list of the benefits you think your friend receives. Are the lists basically balanced? Even within the same friendship, you may find that the benefit balance switches back and forth as time passes. Friendships generally continue as long as the benefits over time are about equal for both individuals. But if you find that there no longer is a balance (for instance, Rebecca's having lots of fun, but Jamie's constantly bored when the two are together), that friendship will probably begin to fall apart. If it's a friendship worth saving, start working on restoring the balance!

UPS AND DOWNS OF FRIENDSHIPS

What can you do to build the friendships you already have? *Communicate!* Talk about what's on your mind. Find out what your friend is thinking, how she feels, what she wants to do. *Make time for your friends!* Include them in your plans. Friendships thrive on time spent together, talking, laughing, sharing. Another way to strengthen the relationship is to put yourself in your friend's place. Try to see things from her perspective as well as your own.

When one person moves away, it's difficult to keep the friendship bond strong. Extra effort is needed to maintain some kind of contact—letters or phone calls can help greatly.

Many traps can break a friendship down. If you find yourself stuck in any of those listed below, get yourself out of the trap. It can hurt both sides of the friendship.

- Gossiping
- Constant criticizing
- Comparing one friend to another in front of others
- Not clearing up misunderstandings
- Lack of communication
- Lack of forgiveness
- Lack of trust
- Using one another instead of really developing the friendship
- Trying to "buy" the friendship

FRIENDSHIP WITH THE "WRONG" FRIENDS

Sometimes you may find yourself with a group of friends who may not be good for you. How do you know if your friends are "wrong" or "right" for you? What's "wrong" for you may be "right" for someone else. But you need to be concerned about what is best for *you*.

If you're in the "wrong" crowd, you may feel that you are not yourself when you're with them. You may feel phoney, that you have to act like them to be liked by them. You can't relax and be yourself. You may feel that you're always trying too hard to be accepted.

Another sign that you're not being true to yourself by being with these people is that you feel constantly pressured—you're not really having fun with them. You may be developing some bad habits that you know are not of benefit to you or anyone else. And you may notice that people in your family are starting to be unusually concerned about who your friends are and what you're doing. These are all signs that can help you think through the quality of your friendships.

With some friends, make up situations of people being in the "wrong" crowd. Show them making decisions and doing something about it. Act out these situations for others who may be dealing with the same issues—perhaps the girls in your troop or group.

BEST FRIENDS—A VERY SPECIAL RELATIONSHIP

Many people have a "best friend." This is usually a person to whom you feel very close, and with whom you can share things you might not tell anyone else. If you could have the ideal best friend, what would that person be like? What qualities would she have? Make a list of characteristics of a best friend who would be ideal for you. Then try to see these qualities in others and try to find them within yourself!

BEING POPULAR

Popularity, like many things in life, has its good points and bad points. It's nice to be liked, to have lots of friends, to be admired by many, but sometimes life can get exhausting if people are constantly pulling you in different directions because they want to be with you. Don't make your life into a popularity contest! If you're popular, fine. If you're not so popular, but have a few close relationships that you feel good about, that's fine too.

If you'd like to be more popular and be the kind of person whom others want as a friend, there are things you can do—it's not a matter of luck. These hints may help:

- Really listen to what others say.
- Initiate conversations.
- Be interesting and fun to be with.
- Pay attention to your appearance.
- Show that you care about others through words and actions.
- Be cheerful and friendly.

GIRL SCOUTING AND FRIENDSHIPS

How does Girl Scouting affect your friendships? Are many of your friends Girl Scouts? Do those girls who are not Girl Scouts know that you are a member? Girl Scouting provides opportunities for girls to make many friends. Perhaps some of your closest friends were found or will be found in Girl Scouting.

However, as an older Girl Scout you are probably well aware that people have different perceptions about what Girl Scouting is—some positive, others negative. You can help them learn more by being Girl Scouting's advocate.

Every Girl Scout can feel good about her membership in the Girl Scout Movement. When friends ask you about Girl Scouting, tell them about the benefits and about some of the exciting aspects of belonging. After hearing what you have to say, they might want to become involved in Girl Scouting too!

A FRIENDSHIP CELEBRATION

There's no better way to celebrate friendship than to have a party! Parties are wonderful for getting to know people better. You can have a party at your house or organize one at a park, beach, skating rink, swimming pool, movie theater, or some other place. The better organized the party is, the more fun it's likely to be.

You will need to discuss your party plans with your family first and get their support and permission. It's also a good idea to have adults nearby *during* the party. Your family should be assured that your friends know that alcohol or drugs are not permitted and that the people coming will treat your home or the place of the party with respect.

Once you have your family's permission and support, you need to make a list of whom you want to invite. You can send written invitations or verbally invite people. Be sure to keep track of who's coming.

Another task is to plan the food. When you know how many people are coming, figure out what types and how much food you will need. As you estimate the amount to get, remember that most people your age have hearty appetites.

Make a list of all the things you'll need: food, utensils, decorations, chairs, etc. After you get everything, do as much preparation as you can ahead of time. After all, you want to be able to have fun at your own party.

You'll have to figure out what people can do at the party. You may want to dance, eat and talk, or play a sport or game. Some parties are built around a theme. For example, if the theme were friendship, you might want to have people tell stories about friendship—about a time they made a new friend, about someone special to them, about something humorous or an exciting adventure they had with a friend.

As the hostess, your job is to make sure your guests feel comfortable and have the opportunity to enjoy themselves. You can greet them as they enter, introduce people to one another, familiarize them with the place of the party, ask them to help themselves to refreshments at a buffet table, and so on.

Be sure to socialize with all of your guests as the party progresses. Encourage people to talk with one another and enjoy themselves.

One reason it is important to have adults around is that they may be needed if things get out of hand. For instance, uninvited strangers may try to crash the party, or people may bring alcohol or drugs. You don't have to tolerate this behavior—you can set the limits. If the people don't do as you ask, get an adult, tell her or him the situation, then let the adult help you deal with the situation.

The main thing is to enjoy your time with your friends and help your friends enjoy themselves. That's why you're there, to celebrate friendship!

FRIEND IN NEED

Friendships are often tested when problems arise or hardships occur. Everyone can think of times when they felt left out or even abandoned when they lost the support of a friend. Today, the old saying "a friend in need is a friend indeed" can still remind you to show your friendship in ways both big and small.

Think about situations where you can help your friends. Role-play situations where your support may require understanding, action, even courage. What would you do if one of your friends . . .

- was harshly criticized by another
- started to experiment with drugs
- mentioned that a family member had physically abused her
- didn't have any money for a new outfit for the school dance
- seemed to be depressed and hinted that suicide could be a solution to her problem
- could not join the group for an outing because she had to take care of her younger brothers

PEER PRESSURE

Your peers are people who are your age, or are similar to you in ability or some other way. They may be members of your Girl Scout troop, other friends, or your classmates. If you've ever let your peers talk you into doing something you weren't sure about or didn't want to do, you've experienced peer pressure.

Peer pressure has its good points. It can help you overcome your fears, encourage you to learn new things, and build your feelings of self-worth. However, it can also make you feel confused, lower your self-esteem, get you in trouble, and lead you to waste a lot of your time.

Whether you're being pressured for good or for bad, it's important to pay attention to how you really feel and what you really want to do—to listen to your own inner voice. It may also help to think about what can happen if you follow one course of action rather than another. Think of what you would do in the following situation:

Your friend's parents go away for the weekend and your friend decides to invite a few people over. (Her parents had given her permission to have friends over when they're away.) She invites you to come over for the get-together. She says she'll have pizza and people will eat, talk, and listen to music. When you get there, there are some people you know and others you don't. Everyone's eating pizza and talking, having a pleasant time. After a while you notice that many of the guests have started drinking beer and some are beginning to get drunk. When the drinkers ask you if you want a drink, what do you do?

At this point, it's time for you to listen to your inner voice. Think of as many possible results as you can for each possible response.

If I say "yes," then . . .

- I might feel grown up.
- I might get into trouble.
- These people might like me more.
- I might have a good time.
- My family might find out.
- I might get sick.
- Some of my friends might think I'm "cool."
- I might not like it.
- I might not respect myself for giving in to peer pressure.

If I say "no," then . . .

- I might respect myself more.
- My friends might think I'm a baby.
- I might feel that I've done the right thing.
- I might have helped others say no, too.
- I might have a better time at the party.
- My friends might respect me more for doing what I want to do.
- My family might be proud of me.

Thinking and feeling things through before you act will help you make decisions you feel good about making. Whatever you decide and however you act, you can learn from what you do.

As noted earlier, peer pressure has another side. It can inspire growth and happiness. This is Yolanda's story:

In the big city where Yolanda grew up, she'd been a Girl Scout since she was eight years old. She had been planning to become a Senior Girl Scout next year, but then she found out that her family was moving to a small town where she didn't know anybody.

After Yolanda's family moved and was settled in the town, Yolanda started going to Girl Scout meetings again. She got along well with the girls and developed some special friendships. There was only one problem—the group she joined loved to go camping. Yolanda had never gone camping before and she was scared.

Now the girls wanted to plan a camping trip and they really hoped Yolanda would go too.

At first, she told them she wouldn't go because she didn't like camping. Then she told them she was really afraid to go and that she had never gone before. Then came the peer pressure—but in a supportive and positive way. Yolanda's Girl Scout friends respected the fact that she was afraid, but then asked her to give them a chance to help her learn more about camping. They told Yolanda all about the fun camping trips they had taken before, showed her pictures and films, gave her books to read about camping, and helped her develop camping skills.

The more Yolanda learned, the less afraid she was of camping. Eventually, she became actively involved in planning the trip and when it was time to go she was actually very enthusiastic. Yolanda and her new friends had a wonderful time camping and Yolanda is eagerly looking forward to future camping trips.

In Yolanda's case, peer pressure helped her to overcome her fears, learn new skills, and discover a new world. In any case, when you face peer pressure remember to listen to your inner voice, follow your feelings, and think through the possible results of your behavior.

Dating

"Did you have a good time?" your best friend asks when she calls up the day after your date.

"It was wonderful."

"I'm in love."

"I'm never going to speak to him again."

"It was so much fun."

"I've never met anyone so boring."

"We laughed all evening."

"He and I have so much in common. We talked for hours."

These are some of the ways you might describe a date. Some dates are exciting experiences, while others are a waste of time. Following are some questions you and your friends may have asked, thought about, or discussed.

WHY DO PEOPLE DATE?

Dating can provide opportunities for fun, sharing, affection, maybe even love. Going to the beach or a movie, watching television or going on a picnic—all can be great fun with a terrific date.

Girls can learn more about boys, what being in a relationship means, and what qualities are important in a partner. Dating can eventually help prepare an individual for choosing a spouse.

In some groups, dating is a way to gain status. For instance, Alyssa dates Matthew because he's the captain of the football team and very popular in school. Is this a good reason for dating someone?

WHY IS DATING OFTEN SO DIFFICULT?

Most girls are somewhat shy or nervous when they first begin to date. They may worry that they won't know what to say or how to act. As girls have more experience dating, these feelings of insecurity usually lessen. Remember, boys have the same kinds of concerns.

You may be afraid of rejection—what if you really like him but he doesn't like you? Or the opposite could happen. After one or two dates, you might decide that you'd like to remain as friends, but that you have no romantic interest in him. Unfortunately he acts as if he's crazy about you. How can you let him know that you'd like to be just friends? It's not easy. Discuss or role-play these situations with some friends.

DECISIONS ABOUT DATING

Some girls begin to date when they're twelve or thirteen, others not until they're eighteen or older. There's no right time to start. Sandra may be emotionally and socially ready to begin dating when she's in the eighth grade while her best friend, Sherry, may not be ready until she's finished high school.

Don't feel pressured into going out with someone just because:

- someone has asked you out
- your friends think you should because he's popular
- your family thinks he's a nice boy

Consider your own feelings, your values, and your needs. How does your family feel about your starting to date? You might want to talk to both your friends and family about dating.

WHAT DO YOU LOOK FOR IN A DATE?

Just as you're not friends with everyone, you're not going to want to date every boy you know. Think about the qualities that are important to you. Remember that appearance doesn't tell you very much about a boy's personality or intelligence. For instance, someone who is very good-looking may also be a real snob. On the other hand, a person might be not only cute, but also friendly and considerate.

Try to give boys who aren't naturally handsome a chance. Sometimes, when you get to know someone, looks become less important. And you may find that the boy who is not particularly nice-looking in seventh grade may surprise you with his attractive looks later on.

Think about your interests, values, and dreams for the future. Wouldn't it be nice to date someone with whom you can share these?

HOW DO BOYS FEEL ABOUT DATING?

Boys, like girls, can feel pressured to date, worry about rejection, and are concerned about how they look and act. But boys often hide their emotions so you may not always know how they really feel. Also, boys may seem to be self-centered when they're actually feeling unsure of themselves. They want to make a good impression, they want to be accepted, and they want to be liked. Sometimes they do things because they think it's expected of them, not because they feel they're ready for the experience.

Boys don't like being used or manipulated. Treat them the way you want to be treated. Act interested only if you really are. Don't act interested in one boy just to meet his friend or to make someone else jealous.

What do boys look for in a date? Probably most of the same qualities girls want—someone who is friendly, considerate, intelligent, self-confident, attractive, kind, supportive, and has a good sense of humor.

HOW CAN YOU SAY "NO" WHEN YOUR DATE SAYS "YES"?

One of the most difficult and emotional issues that comes up related to dating concerns sexual activity. This issue is more likely to present itself with couples who are seeing each other often than with those who have only dated once or twice.

Girls need to be aware of some of the possible consequences of becoming sexually active at a young age.

- Feelings of guilt for going against moral or religious values.
- Problems with parents.

- The trauma of finding out that someone did not share your expectations of future commitment.
- Unwanted pregnancy. (Over 1 million teenage girls get pregnant each year.)
- Sexually transmitted diseases ranging from gonorrhea to AIDS.

Here are some specific ways you can support your decision to say no.

- Avoid situations where you might feel pressured to have sex. (For example, Vincent has asked you to watch television at his house when his parents are away, or Cliff asks you to drive down to the lake with him at midnight.)
- Remember that you always have the right to say no (*even* if you said yes before), and think ahead about how you're going to say it.
- Practice saying "no" by role-playing with friends or by saying no in other situations (for instance, when a classmate asks to copy your homework).
- Avoid dating older boys or men, who generally expect more from girls and may apply more pressure.
- Go out with groups of boys and girls or double date.
- Don't agree to have sex just because you don't want to hurt a boy's feelings. Saying no to sex doesn't have to mean rejecting him as a person.
- Be honest right from the start in your dating relationships. Let your date know your real feelings about sexual activity both through your words and your actions.

Marriage and Parenthood

As an adult you may decide to remain single or you may decide to marry. You may wish to have a family of your own. One of the foundations of a healthy family is a strong and supportive relationship between two people. This is not an easy thing to create, as today's high divorce rates show. However, it is possible; there are many couples who are happy together.

Choosing a mate and raising children are two decisions that affect a person's life tremendously. There are great rewards when people wait until they are emotionally ready and financially able to make the above decisions. There is a greater chance that the decisions made will be successful ones.

What does it mean to be emotionally and financially ready to choose a husband and perhaps have children? For choosing a husband, it means such things as:

- You are ready to stand on your own, to be independent.
- You have a good sense of who you are; you know what you want out of life.
- You are ready to share your life with another person.

For having children, being emotionally and financially ready means that you and your husband:

- Are prepared to make the social, emotional, financial, time, and other sacrifices necessary for successful parenthood.
- Can afford to support a child.

■ Understand and will work to develop the qualities that are important for parenting:

Capacity to love and be loved
Ability to teach
Knowledge about the physical and social worlds
Warmth
Sense of fun and adventure
Empathy
Patience

All of these things take time and experience to develop. Even with a good foundation, the relationships among parents and children need continued love, understanding, and effort to keep them strong.

Unfortunately, too many young women do not wait until they are emotionally and financially ready to choose a spouse or start a family. Today, 1 out of 10 teenagers in the United States become pregnant every year and nearly half of these pregnancies result in births. These young women are most often left with the responsibility of supporting their children with little, if any, support from the fathers of the babies. This often means having a life of poverty and hardship. These teenagers must find housing, food, transportation, medical care, insurance, schooling, and many other things for their new families. They may quickly realize that not waiting until they were ready comes with a high price.

The pressures are tremendous, and children born to teenage parents are at an increased risk for being abused. Taking care of a baby can be exhausting and frustrating when the individual is doing it primarily alone and before she is really ready for the responsibility. Teenage mothers often report feeling very alone, isolated from their friends, overwhelmed by financial troubles, and old before their time. They usually regret not waiting until they were really ready to choose a spouse and start a family.

Fortunately, because of increased awareness of the problem, there are more supports and organizations where teenage mothers can get help to have successful lives.

Parenting, when an individual is ready for it, comes with many joys. Some of them are:

■ Watching your child develop and accomplish new things.
■ Experiencing the special love between parent and child.
■ The fun of playing with your child.
■ The opportunity to help another human being grow.
■ Sharing all these joys with your spouse.

Talk to people who are parents to find out what they think about parenthood. Be sure to talk with both men and women. Also interview people who have no children. Remember that, for some, remaining childless was not their decision, but rather due to an inability to have children of their own.

As you form your own ideas, values, and attitudes about family life, look for and find couples who have good relationships. Find out what they think makes their relationship work—what makes it special and successful. One of the best ways to learn is by following good examples.

Learn all you can about parenting and children. If you have younger brothers and sisters, you already have some experience. Get to know children by volunteering in a day care center, nursery school, or parent-child program. Spend time baby-sitting. Work on the Child Care and Skills for Living interest projects in *Cadette and Senior Girl Scout Interest Projects*. Talk to mothers who have babies younger than one year old. Observe children when they are playing and interacting with their family and friends.

Being realistic about marriage and parenting can help you to have a successful marriage and be a good parent—when the time is right.

The Power of Relationships

People spend enormous amounts of time and energy dealing with relationships—from planning how to look for a special date to coping with the sorrows of relationships that have soured. From the day you are born, relationships begin to add to your life. Relationships form the framework for life and make everything more meaningful. Maintaining established relationships and building new ones will constantly be a part of your life. Being sensitive to others—respecting their needs, feelings, and rights so that you can operate in harmony and mutual understanding—is a lifelong commitment.

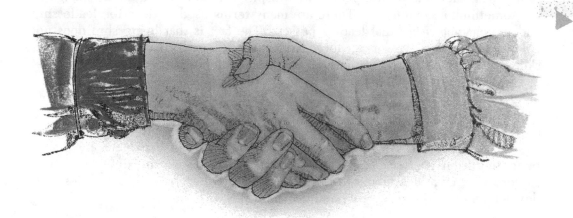

4

LEADERSHIP AND GROUPS

What is leadership? Who are leaders? What do they do? On a very basic level leaders are those people who inspire others to bring about change or get something accomplished. There are many terms used to describe leadership and the characteristics that leaders possess. The fact is that leadership does not fall into one definite type or category, and leaders possess a great variety of talents, skills, and traits that are not the same for every individual.

Leadership isn't confined to just those people who have been elected to office or given an official title. At many different times and in a variety of situations, individuals have the opportunity to be leaders. Leadership skills can be learned and sharpened in Girl Scouting. You can watch what other leaders do, both your friends and the adults involved in your group. And you can learn by doing, benefiting from your successes and your mistakes. Now is the time for you to explore your own ideas about leadership, discover your leadership abilities, and develop and practice leadership abilities and skills.

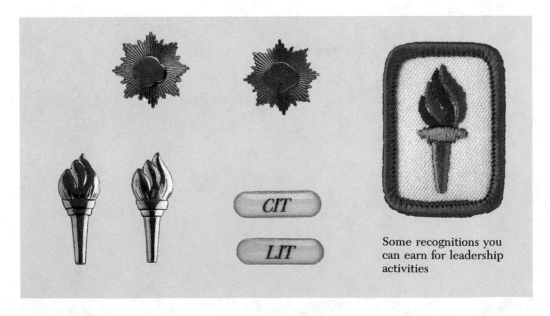

Some recognitions you can earn for leadership activities

Leadership often depends on several things—what must be done, the situation, and what people expect. Each of us, at one time or another, is likely to be in the position of leading a group. Leaders often take on various roles. The roles they

assume may change with time and circumstances and the people with whom they work. Some of these roles are listed below:

director	mediator	problem-solver	motivator
facilitator	guide	confronter	producer
initiator	time-keeper	coach	networker
clarifier	peace-keeper	manager	explorer
listener	nurturer	delegator	dreamer

As a leadership skill building activity, investigate and practice as many of these leadership roles as possible. For example, when you are in a group, practice being a "listener" or a "motivator" or a "networker."

What kinds of qualities do you look for in a leader? Think of four people you know (or know about) whom you would describe as good leaders. For each of these, identify some of the personal qualities that this person has that you admire. Write ten words that describe each of these four people.

Now look at the total picture. Are there similar qualities that you admire in all four leaders? Do you know any people who have some of these characteristics but are not good leaders? Why is this so?

Do the leadership inventory activity in the Leadership interest project, found in *Cadette and Senior Girl Scout Interest Projects*. This inventory lists some of the things leaders do. Which leadership qualities do you have already? Which areas need strengthening? Decide on three ways that you can improve and do something about it.

You and Girl Scout Adults

Your adult partner is your resource in the leadership and management of your group. The leadership roles that adults carry can differ from group to group and can change within the group itself according to the wishes, needs, and experiences of the members. How much direct leadership the adult takes, for example, will depend a lot on how much leadership the other group members are willing and able to carry.

You and adult leaders work together in partnerships aimed at making the most of all your experiences. Adult leaders help you and your group to achieve your goals and to find satisfaction in your efforts and accomplishments. They are there to listen, support, suggest, guide, and act as resources for you as you create the kind of program that best fits your needs and interests.

Group Management

When organizing any sort of group, it is important to keep the group a manageable size and structure. What "manageable" means depends on what you want to do. When the discussion is expected to be general, up to eight or ten participants may be appropriate. However, in groups where you share very personal feelings, a smaller number of people is usually better. Be ready to break into smaller groups when you feel overloaded. When it's to your mutual gain, be willing to join with other subgroups or with outside groups.

Pick the structure for your group that best suits your purpose. Your group may want to use one of the following group structures, or it may create another system that adapts, combines, or is different from any of these.

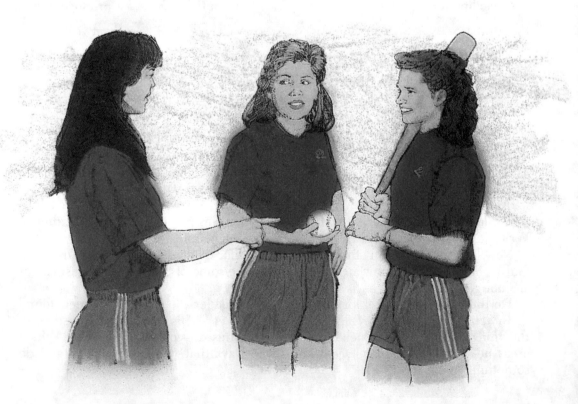

PATROLS

The *patrol system* has always been special to Girl Scouting. It is a representative form of government in which the troop breaks into small groups called patrols. This form of group management works well with large groups, usually 15 or more girls.

Because each patrol is small—usually five to eight members in each—every member can have a say and a chance to try out leadership roles. The patrol leader, elected by the members, has the following responsibilities:

- Conducting regular patrol meetings
- Leading discussions and offering suggestions
- Taking charge of any special assignment given to the patrol
- Assigning duties to patrol members and seeing that they are carried out
- Helping the patrol organize to get jobs done
- Consulting with adult leaders for special help on plans or problems, and keeping them up-to-date on patrol activities
- Representing the patrol at Court of Honor meetings (described below) by reporting on patrol progress and activities, getting needed assistance, and sharing ideas with other patrol leaders

The Court of Honor consists of the adult leader, all patrol leaders, plus a troop treasurer and a troop secretary elected from the total group. At Court of Honor meetings, the patrol leaders voice the ideas and opinions of their patrols, and make decisions and plans that will affect the total group.

EXECUTIVE BOARD

An *executive board* (also known as a steering committee) is a small group within the total group, and is made up of officers (president, vice president, secretary, treasurer, etc.) elected by everyone. This system can be effective for a large group that wishes to have a small, elected representative group serve as the leadership team for everyone.

The executive board gathers ideas from all the members, sorts through them, and recommends some of the activities. It plans and coordinates activities and events for the total group and involves all members in carrying out plans.

The executive board frequently has discussions with the total group and acts as the group's liaison with outside groups. An adult leader acts as adviser to the executive board.

TOWN MEETING

In the *town meeting* system, every member of the group discusses, criticizes, and decides on group business. This system is usually most effective in small groups of less than fifteen.

Moderators may be selected by the total group to guide discussions and help the group arrive at decisions, or members may just take turns carrying out these responsibilities.

Whenever you want to pursue interests or activities that cannot be handled or enjoyed by the total group, a task group or committee may be formed. Committees might investigate information or a particular question, plan and/or carry out parts of a total group project, or carry out routine or special troop tasks.

Effective Groups

As a Girl Scout, you are bound to have the chance to work with different kinds of people who act in different ways. Some people help the group to move forward while others hinder its progress.
A group is helped when someone:

- Energizes people to do more or do better
- Harmonizes situations with humor or soothing words
- Takes care of technical details like supplies, handouts, or room arrangements
- Keeps discussions on target and on time
- Makes sure that no one is feeling left out, that no ideas are overlooked
- Transfers information and inspiration beyond the group so that the group gains support from others
- Opens the group to other people, new ideas, new opportunities

On the other hand, a group may be hindered when someone:

- Makes fun of others' values or feelings
- Interrupts and distracts the group
- Boasts and shows off; tries to take credit for others' efforts
- Is never willing to reach out and try new ideas
- Complains a lot, but never tries to improve things
- Dominates decision-making by acting bossy

Communicating: The Thing Groups Do

To do anything together, you and the other individuals in a group must communicate first. Whether it's through body language or written notes, telephone conversations, posted notices, newsletters, or meetings, the universal thing that groups do is communicate.

As a member of a group, you share ideas, facts, opinions, values, feelings, or needs. There are several methods groups can use to share ideas and generate new ones.

BRAINSTORMING

Brainstorming is a special kind of communication for collecting a lot of ideas in a few minutes. The key is imagination, not practicality or logic, with everyone spilling out whatever ideas come to mind. When brainstorming:

- All ideas are welcome without criticism—that comes later.
- The more inventive the idea, the better.
- Quantity of ideas is what is needed; quality can come later.

Building on others' ideas is welcome in brainstorming. Select a group recorder, someone who can write fast to keep up with the rush of ideas. Or use a tape recorder. Select someone to start and stop the discussion and agree on a signal to use whenever someone makes a judgmental comment such as "That won't work" or "That's silly."

Write the brainstorming subject on a chalkboard or paper that all can see and you're ready to go. When the recorder has collected many ideas, stop and take a look at what you have.

Brainstorming stops when you start judging and choosing ideas to follow through with. Identify ideas your group can use, ideas that do not seem as if they will work for you, and ideas that might turn into something useful, if developed.

Try brainstorming with your friends. How many ideas can you come up with for the following:

- Possible Saturday trips for your group
- Party themes for an evening gathering
- Service projects for the local community
- Activities to do with a group of younger Girl Scouts
- Outdoor adventures that will cost a dollar or less
- Ways of raising money for the troop treasury

DISCUSSION

Group discussion is talking with a purpose. It can help you when you want to exchange ideas, thoughts, and feelings; increase your knowledge about a particular subject; make a decision; or solve a problem. Getting the most out of discussions and using discussion as a step to action take skill and practice on everyone's part.

Here are some guidelines for leading a discussion:

- See that everyone is comfortable. Seat people so that no one feels left out and everyone can see and hear.
- Start by stating the purpose of the discussion as simply and clearly as you can.
- At first—listen. Let the others talk so you can find out if they fully understand the purpose of the discussion.
- Make sure every speaker gets respectful attention.
- In cases where things get noisy and confused, raise your hand for quiet if you are working with other Girl Scouts. Lowering your own voice to a whisper may get everyone's attention back.
- Be prepared with correct information when it is needed, or have a resource nearby with the facts.
- In small groups, try to get the discussion going back and forth among various members rather than from each member to you. In large or more formal groups, all discussion should go through the leader or moderator.
- Summarize the discussion. Repeat the main points that have been made or arguments pro and con and bring an end to the discussion.

PUBLIC PRESENTATIONS

Communicating information often requires that an individual or group of individuals present before a larger group. Depending on the technique used and the type of information presented, the audience may also participate—asking questions, reacting, and commenting. Dramatizations, talks, and panel presentations can be effective means of group communication.

Dramatizations

Skits and role-playing are fine dramatic techniques to try when the group is faced with a difficult problem or situation. Perhaps you are going to meet the public during a money-earning project or conduct interviews to gather information. A few girls can take the parts of people who will be in the situation and, without rehearsal, act it out while the others watch. Then the whole group can talk over what has taken place and what problems may arise.

Dramatization is most likely to be successful when there is a very specific situation or problem to be dramatized. The situation should be clear, not too complicated, and possible for the actors to treat realistically. If the group is really concerned about the problem that is being dramatized, the audience and the actors will take their roles seriously. It will be helpful if at least a few members of the group are prepared to improvise actions and reactions that may actually occur.

Skits and role-playing can be particularly good in communicating ideas and information to younger children. They can be encouraged to participate and usually enjoy such learning situations.

Talks, Public Speaking

Almost everyone at some time or another is requested to give a talk before a group of people. This is an excellent communication skill and one that is perfected through practice, especially before live audiences. During your Cadette and Senior Girl Scout years, you will most likely be asked to talk before or on behalf of your group.

When you give a talk or public presentation:

- Make sure you know the purpose of your presentation and the subject matter it should contain.
- Organize your material. Review what you know and find out more, if necessary. Choose a few main points and arrange them in logical order.
- Be clear and concise, using a conversational tone, simple words, and short, colorful examples to keep people interested. Spontaneous touches of humor always help.
- Use notes if they help you feel comfortable, but try to look at the group most of the time while you are speaking.
- Consider combining the talk with other methods. You might outline the main points on a blackboard or chart for people to follow as you speak.
- If you wish, encourage participation by inviting questions and comments during or after the talk.
- Remember that most people do not retain most of what they hear. After the first five to ten minutes of a talk, retention drops even more. To accommodate this tendency, many public speakers identify the key points in the beginning, then elaborate, and end with a brief summary.

Panels

A panel presentation is another way for people to communicate and share information. It is a planned talk by three to eight people who have special knowledge of a subject and often different points of view. They sit at a table in front of an audience and hold an orderly conversation that is followed by questions and answers and general discussion.

Opening Jitters, Stage Fright, and Silent Panic

One of the first things you need to realize when coping with any fear or anxiety before or during a public presentation is that you are not alone. Just about everyone experiences some degree of anxiety, from mild discomfort to out-and-out panic, when they must speak in front of a group. There's no easy cure. Some people find that practice and experience help; some people never completely lose the fear they feel each time they step in front of an audience. A good deal of your feelings about public speaking will depend on you and your personality. However, there are some tips that can help to lessen your fears.

- Be prepared. Know your stuff. You'll be less likely to make mistakes that will cause you to feel even worse.
- Practice. Try presenting in front of one or two family members or friends. Watch yourself in front of a mirror or, if possible, make an audio- or videotape that you can review.
- Don't try to memorize absolutely everything. If you overmemorize, one slip might cause you to lose your train of thought.
- Scan your eyes over the heads of the audience rather than making eye contact. It will appear that you are addressing them, and this technique will help you avoid feeling overwhelmed by everybody watching you.
- Do something to keep your mind off the presentation until it's time to get ready. Panic can build if you have time to dwell on your

nervousness. While waiting to speak, count backwards from 100, or try to remember the names of everyone in your first-grade class.

■ Try to stand, sit, or move in a relaxed, comfortable manner. Don't try too hard to be formal.

■ Read the stress management section on pages 67–69 for more tips.

■ Remember—you're probably your own hardest critic. The people listening to you don't hear the tremor in your voice or notice the anxiety you feel.

Work Groups and Buzz Groups

At times, subgroups need to be formed to explore segments of larger issues. Breaking off into work groups or buzz groups can be efficient ways to deal with aspects of a broader topic.

Work groups are small discussion groups that deal with some specific topic or project in which its members have a vital interest. These groups can cover more ground more efficiently than would be true if the whole troop worked together at the same time. Work groups give each girl a chance to take active responsibility, and they encourage the natural leadership within the group. A work group may spend several meetings exploring a problem thoroughly. It then reports its solutions or directions for further action to the whole group. For example, a work group might develop a plan for a money-earning project.

Buzz groups should not be confused with work groups. Buzz groups last only a few minutes. They are formed on the spur of the moment to obtain spontaneous reaction to some problem or situation. At the end of their discussion, a reporter from each buzz group tells the group what her buzz group said. For example, a buzz group might consider the pros and cons of meeting on Sundays during March.

Voting and Consensus

Voting and consensus are two ways to close discussion with a decision. Voting can be done by secret ballot, raising hands, standing up, voice, or ballot box. Each vote should be recorded if the outcome is to be pooled with others (for example, if all patrol votes are to be added together to get a single troop vote).

To decide by consensus, the entire group considers alternatives and comes to a decision that all members can support. By considering all points of view, and by combining the best of all alternatives, the group should be able to reach a consensus, an opinion agreed to by all participants.

Parliamentary Procedure

Parliamentary procedure is a way to discuss and decide. This procedure is often used at board meetings, school meetings, government meetings, Girl Scout National Council meetings, and in many other instances. Parliamentary procedure is particularly useful when large groups of people meet.

Parliamentary procedure is a democratic system by which all members of the group are able to express their opinions on an issue or question. Decisions are made by voting or some form of general agreement. To learn more about this method, attend meetings where parliamentary procedure is used in your community or read about it. One well-known book is *Robert's Rules of Order, Newly Revised* by Henry M. Robert. You might also refer to *Parliamentary Procedures at a Glance* by O. Garfield Jones and *Pointers on Parliamentary Procedure* from the National Association of Parliamentarians.

The chart below shows some of the more common terms used in parliamentary procedure.

Term	Meaning
Adjourn	To end a meeting
Agenda	A list of items in the order to be brought up at the meeting
Amendment	A change made to a motion
Division	A call for a standing vote
Majority	More than half of the voters
Minutes	An accurate record of the group's actions and decisions
Motion	A brief statement of a proposed action
Point of information	A request for information or clarification
Point of order	An objection made because of a perceived improper procedure
Quorum	The number of participants eligible to vote needed to conduct a meeting—usually a majority of the group
Standing vote	A vote in which the participants show their position on a question by standing up or raising their hands

Once you have learned about parliamentary procedure, practice using it as a group at some of your Girl Scout meetings.

Organizing for Action

Organizing a group for action requires some specific efforts. This section describes the steps groups need to take to accomplish their goals.

GOAL-SETTING

Setting goals is the first step toward group action. It's also something you do every day, though you may not always call it that. You need to state, "Here is something I want to make happen." And, for an individual or a group, that's what goals are: statements of something you'd like to see happen or exist in the future. When a group sets goals for itself, it enhances the chances for success.

Here are some goal-setting ideas you can use in any group. Put them to work as you head toward group accomplishment.

Make your goal clear—get it in writing—even if it's just on a big piece of paper that everyone can see, agree to, and refer back to as a reminder. Be as specific as you can. (Goals are often stated in terms of "to be _____," "to be able to _____," "to complete by _____.") For example, "Our goal is: To set up and run an after-school reading clinic at Fairfield Library, beginning in February." Or: "Our goal is: To go camping at Clear Lake on the third weekend in June."

Be realistic. Ask yourselves:

■ Are you really interested enough in this goal to spend your time, energy, and money on it?
■ Will you have the support you'll need (parents, Girl Scout council, school consultants)?
■ What difficulties or obstacles will you need to overcome? Can you? Are you ready to?

If your answers make reaching your goal sound impossible, ask yourselves how you might change your goal or the steps for achieving it. Being realistic doesn't have to mean putting aside a cherished dream or accepting second-best. Big things are possible, but they may call for extra effort and imagination.

Mark your path to your goal. Most goals are fairly long-range projections, and you reach them step by step, not all at once. Shorter, in-between steps help you spell out some of the "hows" of reaching your larger goal. For example, our goal is: "To go camping at Clear Lake on the third weekend in June."

Some steps we can take are:

Reserve the campsite.
Check the first-aid kit.
Arrange for transportation.

PLANNING AS A GROUP

Planning ahead can help the group move toward its goal. But don't be afraid to change plans if that seems right. Sometimes lists and charts can help you organize your plans. For example, you might list the following:

What needs to be done?
By when?
How?
Who will do it?
How much will it cost?
Where will the money come from?

The Long-Range Calendar

A long-range calendar is helpful when you need to accommodate a number of different activities into a total group action plan.

To get the big picture, use a calendar to identify the activities that will take place during each month. Place an "M" next to those activities that will take place during the regular meeting times and locations. Place a "T" next to the activities to be done by the total group. Place an "S" next to the activities that will be done by a subgroup.

Here's a sample of months from a calendar for a group that had many interests.

September

Planning meetings (T, M)
Money-earning event (T)
Apply for wider opportunities (S)

October

Camping trip (T)
Cycling interest project (S)
Photography interest project (S)

November

Community service project (T)
Photo exhibit of bicycle trips to combine interest project group
   efforts (S)
Cycling interest project (continued)
Photography interest project (continued)

December

Holiday party (international dinner) (T, M)
Complete interest projects (S)

January

Career Exploration interest project (S)
Cadette Girl Scout Challenge (S)
Auto Maintenance interest project (S)

February

Planning and evaluation (T, M)
Career Exploration interest project (continued)
Cadette Girl Scout Challenge (continued)
Auto Maintenance interest project (continued)

March

Council cookie sale (T)
Fashion and beauty workshop (T)
Service project planning (S)
Complete interest projects (S)

BALANCING THE LOAD: DELEGATING RESPONSIBILITY

Delegating responsibilities is a matter of dividing whatever needs to be done into various jobs, describing responsibilities, and making assignments. It may help to consider job titles for people who will lead or coordinate, direct the action, get things ready, get the job done, clean up, evaluate, or do follow-up activities.

When delegating responsibility, try to assign people the types of jobs they do best. However, it is also important to balance the load, making sure that everyone gets an opportunity to cooperate and participate, developing skills as both followers and leaders.

Here are a few questions to consider when you look for balance:

- Are the same people doing most of the work?
- Is there a balance between the responsibilities of girls and adults?
- Are assignments specific enough? (Everyone's job can turn out to be no one's if assignments are not clear.)

Record-Keeping

Records are especially helpful when your group wants to recall past efforts and evaluations, answer questions about time and money, plan ahead and

monitor progress, make agreements and share results, pass on information to new members. When preparing records, remember to:

■ Keep your notes together, not just in your head or on loose bits of paper.
■ Organize your notes. Use symbols to alert you to special items. An asterisk might mean decisions to be made; a check mark could indicate new business to report.
■ Be sure all facts are complete and correct.

Developing an Agenda

An agenda, an orderly list of things to be done in a meeting, can help the meeting run smoothly. Keep these ideas in mind:

■ Decide on the order of items, keeping related ones together.
■ Set approximate time limits for each topic.
■ Share the proposed agenda with members and get their input.

Be sure to follow the agenda at the meeting. Toward the end of the meeting, ask for agenda items for the next meeting.

Note-Taking

It's a good idea to have one member responsible for taking notes during or shortly after a meeting. These notes, often called minutes, can serve as a record of decisions reached, areas of disagreement, and future plans. Remember to note:

■ Decisions and general agreements
■ The number of votes for and against an issue (especially important if your group's votes will be added to others for the final outcome)
■ How jobs were divided, who was responsible for what, and any suggestions for improvement

Reporting back, updating absent members, and building the next agenda all are made easier by complete and accurate note-taking.

Budgeting

Some of what your group does and the plans you make will depend on money. Recording and projecting your needs and the cash required to meet those needs is basically what a budget is all about.

Here is a sample worksheet to help you plan a budget for a year. First, figure out your proposed outgo—how much you plan to spend. You might consider the following things.

Proposed Outgo

Girl Scout Annual Membership Dues
(National dues multiplied by number of girls in the group) $_____

Meeting Equipment
(Do you need things like a new bulletin board, or supplies for the first-aid kit?) $_____

Resources
(How much are the books or other materials you'd like?) $_____

Continuing Program
(Will you need money for service projects, activities with other Girl Scouts, or other long-term plans?) $_____

Flexible Program
(Money for spur-of-the-moment ideas) $_____

Special Events
(Camping, trips, councilwide events) $_____

    $_____

    $_____

Total Proposed Outgo $_____

To find out how much money will have to be allotted for each girl, divide the total proposed outgo by the number of girls in the troop/group.

Next, figure out a plan to get the group income to match the proposed outgo.

Expected Income

Troop/Group Dues $_____

Cookie/Product Sales Revenue $_____

Troop Money-Earning Projects $_____

Total Expected Income $_____

See page 118 for ways to carry out troop or group money-earning projects. Remember, your troop or group needs written permission from your council before starting a money-earning project. A worksheet will help you explain what the money will be used for.

Leadership in Girl Scouting

Cadette Girl Scout
Leadership Award

You will have many opportunities to develop your leadership skills in Girl Scouting. There are a number of recognitions you may earn, including the Cadette Girl Scout Leadership Award and the Senior Girl Scout Leadership Award. Your council may also have set up numerous leadership opportunities. Among the possibilities are Cadette or Senior planning boards, advisory boards, congresses, and assemblies in which girls take part in developing councilwide activities or get involved in the decision-making process of their council. Senior Girl Scouts may also serve on standing committees of the council board of directors, and some Senior Girl Scouts serve on the standing committees of the National Board of Directors. Find out what options already exist in your council. Your adult partner can assist you in finding more information. For example, you may become a program aide, a Leader-in-Training (LIT), a Counselor-in-Training (CIT), or an apprentice trainer.

Senior Girl Scout
Leadership Award

PROGRAM AIDE

As a program aide you can work directly with a troop or camp unit of younger girls under the supervision of an adult volunteer or staff member. It's an opportunity to share your valuable experience with sister Girl Scouts as they work on exciting projects and important issues. Talk to your leader or contact your council office for more information.

Girl Scout
Silver Award

LEADER-IN-TRAINING OPPORTUNITIES

You can also serve in a leadership capacity as a Leader-in-Training (LIT). This volunteer service will be developed by your own council or, in some instances, with another council or Girl Scout group. However, there are general guidelines that all LIT projects should include.

Girl Scout
Gold Award

Leader-in-Training Guidelines

A Leader-in-Training completes a group leadership course, either before or during her work as an assistant leader of a Daisy, Brownie, Junior, or Cadette Girl Scout troop. An LIT project extends over a five- to eight-month period, with the time divided between course sessions and actual work with a troop or other Girl Scout group.

To qualify to be a Leader-in-Training, you must:

- be a registered member of Girl Scouts of the U.S.A.;
- be at least 14 years of age or entering ninth grade;
- have demonstrated interest in working with children; and
- have a real interest in the progress and welfare of younger Girl Scouts.

As an LIT applicant you should discuss your needs, interests, and qualifications with a Girl Scout leader to determine your readiness for an LIT project and to learn about the council application procedures.

Leader-in-
Training pin

Counselor-in-
Training pin

Leadership
interest project
patch

57

LIT Course Content

Although the exact length and structure of the group leadership course are flexible and determined by your council and the trainers involved, LIT training includes the following topics:

- An understanding of basic Girl Scout values as stated in the Promise and Law and the four program emphases
- Troop/group business, including finances, bank accounts, troop records, and permission and sponsorship forms
- The basics of child development and how children learn
- Methods for working with youngsters with special needs
- An overview of the basic Girl Scout program resources for the age level with which you will be working
- Council fund-raising efforts like Girl Scout cookie and calendar sales
- Special council projects and events that may add to the general Girl Scout program
- Progression in the out-of-doors, including camping
- Group dynamics and leadership

Working with Adult Partners

Your placement as an LIT should meet your needs as well as those of the troop and leader with whom you are placed. The individuals responsible for supervising LIT projects in your council can identify leaders who can successfully function as your adult partners.

As you intern with a younger troop as an LIT, adult guidance will be provided to help you evaluate your leadership ability on a continuing basis.

While serving as an LIT, you may wear an LIT position pin above your membership pin. Like the yellow position pin worn by adult leaders, it signifies your important role in Girl Scouting.

LIT Course Evaluation

Evaluation is an essential component of the Leader-in-Training course. The evaluation process helps determine the success of the project and provides a focus for future plans.

Your evaluation should include the following questions:

- Did you develop and strengthen your leadership skills?
- Did the training meet your personal goals?
- What changes can or should be made in future LIT projects?

COUNSELOR-IN-TRAINING OPPORTUNITIES

Counselor-in-Training (CIT) opportunities are developed by your own council or by another Girl Scout council or group. Following are the CIT guidelines.

Counselor-in-Training Guidelines

A Counselor-in-Training project offers older Girl Scouts the opportunity to work with children in the out-of-doors and to acquire valuable on-the-job experience. A Counselor-in-Training completes an outdoor group leadership course while interning as a counselor in a Girl Scout camp. The training includes regular hours devoted to classes, plus actual experience in camp units where the Counselor-in-Training works directly with the children under the direct supervision of a camp counselor or unit leader.

Participation in a CIT course should help you better understand the essential elements of Girl Scout program and the objectives and philosophy of outdoor education, camping, and leadership; develop your ability to share knowledge, skills, and experiences in group living; and promote positive attitudes toward your responsibilities.

To qualify as a Counselor-in-Training, you must:

- meet all the qualifications for a Leader-in-Training;
- have enough experience in camping skills to be able to teach them to others;
- have accrued at least eight weeks of resident, core, or day camp experience, or four weeks of camp plus other comparable experience acceptable to the council; and
- have serious intentions of becoming a camp counselor or camp specialist.

As a CIT applicant you should discuss your needs, interests, and qualifications with a Girl Scout leader to determine your readiness and to learn about the council application procedures.

CIT Course Content

Although the exact CIT course length and structure are determined by your council and the trainers involved, the CIT course content includes the following topics:

- A review of Girl Scout program resources, especially *Outdoor Education in Girl Scouting*
- A review of basic Girl Scout values as stated in the Promise and Law and the four program emphases, as well as basic Girl Scout principles and practices such as girl planning, girl/adult partnership, the organization and makeup of a Girl Scout troop, troop government, troop activities, and progression in skill building
- A discussion of the Girl Scout organization, including the council and national structures, goals and objectives, and the relationship of the camp to its council
- Group dynamics and leadership
- The history, philosophy, and objectives of camping in Girl Scouting, trends in camping, information about the council's camps and program activities
- Career opportunities in outdoor education
- The specific skills and knowledge needed for campcraft, sports activities, creative activities, and environmental education, with emphasis on the leadership role
- Camp government, including the patrol system, town meetings, special committees, and camp council; basic principles of administration, including planning, organizing, delegating, supervising, and evaluating
- Camp management, covering administration and operation, site

management, camp maintenance and repair, business procedures, records and reports, supplies and inventory
■ The basics of child development, to promote knowledge and understanding of girls between the ages of 5 and 17
■ Safety education, including risk management, Girl Scout program and camping standards, first aid and cardiopulmonary resuscitation (CPR) training, and knowledge of applicable federal, state, and local laws and regulations

Visits to day, core, and resident camps run by various groups are also part of your training as a CIT. Observing how different types of camps are operated can provide you with valuable information.

While serving as a CIT, you may wear the yellow CIT position pin above your membership pin. The CIT pin signifies your important role in Girl Scouting.

Evaluation

The evaluation at the end of the CIT course should include the following questions:

■ Did the training meet your individual goals?
■ Did the training strengthen your leadership skills and knowledge of group dynamics?
■ Did the training help you to determine whether you can be an effective camp counselor?
■ How did this project benefit the camp at which you worked?
■ What changes can or should be made for future CIT projects?

APPRENTICE TRAINERS

Senior Girl Scouts who have completed an LIT project may gain further leadership experience by becoming apprentice trainers. See page 160 for more information.

Recognitions for Leadership

Remember that you can earn Girl Scout recognitions for your leadership experiences, as outlined on pages 143–144 and 152–153. Take advantage of the numerous leadership opportunities Girl Scouting provides and make your leadership potential turn into a reality.

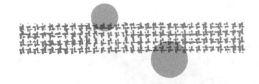

5

LIFE SKILLS

These days, you are probably making many decisions about how you look and act. This is a time of testing and experimenting: what types of food and exercise seem best for you, what type of clothing you prefer, what you'll do with your friends, what ways you'll find to deal with stress. Sometimes your decisions will be easy and other times your choices will be important ones that are quite difficult.

As you take on more and more control of your daily life, you move closer to the independence of being an adult. The range of skills that you will need will vary from the simple to the complex. This chapter explores some of those skills for living that you will find helpful now and throughout your life.

Finding the Road to Health and Fitness

The way you take care of yourself now will affect you for the rest of your life. Good health and fitness habits established early in life often continue into adulthood and lead to a more active and healthy lifestyle.

This section will help to answer some of your questions about your changing body and how to care for it, the right foods to eat, and how to feel your best. This information can help you find the road to health and fitness.

WHAT'S HAPPENING TO YOUR BODY?

Understanding why your body functions as it does, and realizing what is normal for you are important. During the ages of nine through 16, puberty, many mental and physical changes take place.

The rate and extent of these changes vary from person to person. You've probably noticed that not everyone changes in the same ways at the same time. Whether you're changing faster or slower than others, there's no need to worry. When you ask yourself "Am I normal?", it's important to remember that no two people are alike—what's normal for you may not be for someone else. That's why you must be in touch with how *your* body and mind function.

You are also changing emotionally and intellectually. You are capable of learning much more and you are able to reason and think at a more complex and sophisticated level. Your feelings and moods may change more rapidly. You may be happy one moment and sad the next, and not really know why. You may be more aware of your sexual feelings and may feel anxious and nervous around boys.

Curiosity and concern about all the changes your body is going through are natural.

■ Talk with a parent, other relative, or adult whom you trust about how she felt about this stage of her life. You might ask her what changes she noticed first and at what age, how she felt, and what she remembers most about that time.

■ Find out about the types of changes boys experience during puberty.

■ For six months, keep a record of your menstrual cycle and any physical or psychological signs (for example, oilier hair, acne, moodiness) you notice during this time. Note on a calendar the day your period begins and the day it ends. Calculate how often it comes and how many days it lasts.

■ Have a group discussion on questions and concerns about the physical or emotional experiences of maturing. Each girl writes a question or concern she has on a piece of paper. The group tries to answer each question by telling what advice they would give and why. Check out the advice given with a parent, physician, school nurse, or other adult whom you trust.

EATING THE RIGHT FOODS

What you eat has an effect on your physical health, appearance, and emotions. Food supplies energy, builds and repairs tissues, and helps regulate bodily processes. The amount of energy that your body gets from the food you eat is measured in calories. Girls from ages 12 to 18 usually need about 2,000 to 2,500 calories a day. These caloric requirements should be supplied by a balanced diet. Carbohydrates, proteins, fats, vitamins, and minerals are the five major nutrients, and along with water, are essential for a healthy body. Eating right means selecting a variety of foods each day from the four food groups. These groups include: fruits and vegetables; cereals and breads; milk and dairy products; and meats and other protein. During your teen years, your needs for these nutrients are especially high.

To lose weight, you must reduce the number of calories you consume each day and to gain weight you would increase your intake of calories. A weight chart can tell you what is the right weight for you depending upon your height and body frame.

■ Compare the calorie contents of your favorite foods or snacks. Look in a calorie counter book for this information. You may be surprised by some of the amounts.

■ Find out how each nutrient helps the body grow and which foods contain each nutrient. Plan a meal that includes all of these nutrients.

Many foods are high in empty calories. These foods usually have high fat or sugar content. Your body is getting a lot of calories but they aren't very helpful in building your body. That's why healthy eating means eating nutritious snacks (apples, carrots, celery, raisins) and avoiding those that contain high calories but no or few nutrients (soft drinks, chips, candy, pastries). Drinking several glasses of water each day is important for the healthy functioning of your organs. The Creative Cooking interest project will give you ideas on combining nutritious eating with good cooking skills.

Eating right also means being careful not to overeat or undereat. Stay away from fad diets. They usually don't work or the lost weight is easily regained. Losing a large amount of weight in a short period of time can be dangerous to your health. Be sure to get advice from a doctor before dieting. Many girls who have negative views about their bodies fear gaining weight or becoming fat. This may lead to two eating disorders called anorexia and bulimia.

People with anorexia eat very little and often exercise too much. They usually get very thin, but still consider themselves not thin enough. People with bulimia binge—eat large amounts of food at one time—and then purge—force themselves to vomit. Both of these disorders can lead to serious health problems if treatment is not received by a health care professional. If you know someone who seems to have anorexia or bulimia, try to get her to see a doctor or go to a counseling center. See *Girls Are Great*, GSUSA's Contemporary Issues booklet on growing up female, for more information.

SMOKING, ALCOHOL, AND DRUGS

Cigarettes, alcohol, and drugs are used by many young people for different reasons—to look grown-up; to avoid pressure from peers; to satisfy curiosity; to relieve boredom, depression, or anxiety; to rebel against parents, teachers, or others in authority; to deal with stress in the home or school. In most areas of the country, these substances are readily available or relatively easy to obtain. The fact is, they are all harmful to the body. Using and abusing these substances is a serious threat to your health and well-being, and once you've gotten hooked on a substance, the habit can be very difficult to break.

Don't risk becoming a smoker, problem drinker, or drug abuser. If you want to feel good about yourself and in control of your own well-being, say no to drugs.

SHAPING UP

Being physically fit means being able to perform daily tasks vigorously with energy left over for enjoying leisure time activities. Physical fitness involves the performance of the heart and lungs, and the muscles of the body. Fitness also influences to some degree your alertness and the way you feel emotionally.

Physical fitness is influenced by a number of factors including your age, sex, heredity, personal habits, and exercising and eating practices.

Different exercises affect your fitness in different ways. Exercise can strengthen and tone muscles, improve flexibility, and strengthen the heart and lungs. Some popular forms of exercise are swimming, cycling, aerobic dance, yoga, brisk walk-

ing, and jogging. For best results and to avoid personal injuries, exercise programs should (1) begin slowly and build gradually, (2) include a period of warm-up and cool-down, and (3) be carried out regularly.

One way to make exercise a regular daily habit is to choose physical activities that can fit into your lifestyle. The chart below lists some forms of physical activities you may enjoy and their benefits.

Physical Activity	Fitness Benefits
Aerobic dance	Conditions heart and lungs; develops rhythm, agility, and coordination.
Swimming	Conditions total body, tones muscles, relaxes body.
Bicycling	Conditions heart and lungs, strengthens leg and back muscles.
Walking (brisk)	Lowers resting heart rate, improves oxygen consumption, reduces blood pressure.
Running/jogging	Conditions heart and lungs, tones muscles, increases stamina.
Volleyball	Builds muscular strength, speed, power, hand-eye coordination, and agility.
Softball	Builds muscular strength, speed, agility, and coordination.

If you are overweight, easily fatigued, physically inactive, an excessive smoker, or have a personal or family history of health problems, it is strongly recommended that you have a complete physical examination before beginning an exercise program.

Fitness Activities

Decide on a fitness activity you can participate in for 30 minutes to one hour at least three times a week. Try the activity for three months. Keep a record of your progress.

Here are some other fitness activities to try:

■ Take the stairs instead of the elevator or escalator whenever possible. Walk to and from school, a friend's house, or a nearby store. Take your dog for a long stroll.
■ Sign up for a course in swimming, tennis, or aerobics.
■ Put on your dancing shoes and dance a while. Fast dancing burns about 450 calories per hour.
■ Organize a bike hike with several friends or family members. Plan and do a practice run of the route beforehand. Prepare maps for everyone and take along water or fruit juice for a break. Do some warm-up and cool-down exercises before and after the hike. Take some healthy snacks along to eat after the cool-down exercises.

Staying in shape offers you many benefits. They include:

■ Looking, feeling, and performing better
■ Increased strength, endurance, and coordination
■ Improved functioning of your lungs, heart, blood vessels, and digestive system
■ Reduced stress and tension
■ Reduced chronic fatigue

Why not make a personal commitment to get in the habit of staying in shape?

CHECK-UPS

Going to the doctor for regular check-ups will give you an opportunity to stay informed about your state of health and to ask questions about any health matters that concern you. A doctor can help you set up a health care schedule that's right for you.

You will also need a physical examination to participate in swimming, hiking, or other strenuous activities in Girl Scouting.

The You Everybody Sees

Feeling terrific about yourself can have a lot to do with the way you look. Your clothes, your hairstyle, and perhaps the makeup you wear can be a means of expressing your personality and tastes.

CLOTHING

Having suitable clothes for all the different occasions and activities in your life isn't easy, especially when your money is limited. Remember to consider that you are growing fast, that certain colors will suit you best, and that the ways you spend your time should influence your purchase decisions.

Decide how to get the most from the clothes you already have. For example, put outfits together in different combinations; add an interesting accessory like a pin or a scarf. Next decide what you need to buy to round out your wardrobe. When shopping for clothes, ask yourself these questions:

Is this for *me*? Is it becoming to my face and figure?

Will I get good use from it?

Is the price within my budget?

Will it go with things I already own?

Does it fit properly?

Can it be laundered? Is it preshrunk?

Does it seem likely to wrinkle or fade?

Is the style right for my age and usual activities?

Will I still like it a month from now?

Can it be worn for more than one season of the year?

Try visiting clothing outlets and warehouses that sell brand-name clothing at substantial discounts. Look through newspapers for bargains and special sales. (Many stores have end-of-season sales.)

Here are some activities to try:

- Have a fashion show around a theme and have other girls model the appropriate clothing.
- Select one or two items of clothing that you have grown tired of and decide how you might recycle them.
- Complete some activities from the Fashion/Fitness/Makeup interest project.
- Swap clothes with friends or family members.

MAKEUP

The decision to wear makeup is a personal one. Many people choose not to use any makeup; others may use just lipstick or eye makeup. Makeup can enhance your attractiveness, highlight your best features, and soften your flaws. Using it depends on when you are ready and when your parents or guardians give you permission to use it.

Here are some tips on makeup:

- Cleanse your face before applying makeup.
- Match your natural skin tones.
- Avoid too much makeup.
- Ask others for their opinion as to what looks best.

- Be careful not to use eye makeup too close to the inside of your eye.
- Never share makeup with others. You can easily spread bacteria.
- Never go to bed without taking off your makeup. Use a cleanser that is right for your skin type.
- Use deeper shades at night or for special occasions.

Looking good for yourself is more important than trying to look like or please someone else. Be happy with the special person you see each day in the mirror.

HAIRSTYLES

Your hairstyle should be attractive for you and make you feel good about yourself. Here are some tips to help you decide how to style your hair. Consider:

- The shape of your face and its bone structure—your face may be round, long, square, oval, or heart-shaped
- The length of your neck—short or long
- Your figure—heavy, tall, slender, or petite

Keeping the above factors in mind, select two or three hairstyles that suit your overall look. Health and beauty magazines may be a helpful source.
For more information and activities on looking your best:

- Look through beauty and health magazines for ideas.
- With your troop/group, plan and conduct a beauty workshop. Invite consultants to demonstrate proper care of skin, hair, and teeth, and how to apply makeup. Ask them to give diet and shape-up tips.
- Make your own cleansing facial for a refreshed look. Mix one tablespoon of raw bran (available in supermarkets and health-food stores) with two tablespoons of plain yogurt and one teaspoon of wheat germ or vegetable oil. Mix to form a thick paste and apply with your fingertips, using gentle, circular motions. The bran helps shed dead skin cells, the rich oil lubricates, and the yogurt cleanses, cools, and tightens.
- Try some activities from the Fashion/Fitness/Makeup interest project.

Stress Management

There are many things you can do to change your mood when you're feeling depressed, bad about yourself, or under stress. Stress refers to the influences and demands placed on you and your physical, emotional, and mental responses. Stress isn't always bad—it can be created by either good or bad things that happen in life.
Each individual responds differently to stress and can tolerate a different amount of stress. Stress overload is too much stress for you to deal with and makes you feel tense, frustrated, or anxious.

Long

Square

Oval

Round

Heart-shaped

Here are some bodily responses you may have noticed when you are under stress:

- Heart beats faster
- Breathing becomes quicker
- Stomach feels as if it's in knots
- Excessive sweating
- Mouth becomes dry and swallowing is more difficult
- Tight feeling in chest

Try to identify the sources of stress in your own life and, if possible, begin to deal with them in a positive and healthy manner. The inability to handle stress can lead to chronic headaches, depression, or harmful or self-destructive behavior such as compulsive drinking or drug taking, running away, and even suicide attempts.

Make a daily stress log for one week, recording the time, the event that caused the stress, your feelings, and your behavior. This log can help you determine what events are stressful for you and how you handle them. At the end of the week, review your log and list any patterns of times or events. Are there any situations you might be able to handle differently? If you can't come up with any ideas, ask a trusted adult or friend.

Here are some ideas about what you can do when you are under stress. Add your own suggestions to this list as you begin to understand how stress affects you.

- Try exercising or doing some other physical activity like jogging, walking, dancing, or bicycling.
- Read a funny book, see a funny movie. Sometimes it's true that laughter is the best medicine.

- Talk to a friend, family member, teacher, or member of the clergy.
- Don't try to solve problems that are beyond your control. Accept that there are some problems you will not be able to change, at least not immediately.
- Get enough rest and learn to relax (one way to relax is described below).
- Make time for fun by taking a break daily.
- Write in a personal diary or journal.
- Try not to accomplish too many tasks at once. Make a list of what you want to do and complete one task at a time. Mark off the tasks as you complete them.
- Cry, if this will relieve your tension. Sometimes a good healthy cry can bring immediate relief from feelings of stress.
- Find a hobby you enjoy.

RELAXATION

One of the best strategies for avoiding stress is learning how to relax. Below is one technique to help you relax. Dress in loose, comfortable clothing. Find a quiet place, lie flat on your back on a mat or carpeted floor, close your eyes, and concentrate on nothing.

Have your leader or other adult read these instructions while you and the girls in your group follow them.

Fantasy Trip

1. You are about to take a vacation. Imagine yourself in a place you enjoy—a sunny beach, a boat on a lake, or a ski slope.
2. Enjoy the feel of the sun, the sand or snow underneath, or a fresh breeze.
3. Use your senses. Capture the sounds of the trees, the birds, wind and water. Smell the different fragrances in the air.
4. Imagine yourself doing something you really enjoy like reading a book, writing a letter, or floating in calm water.
5. Spend about ten minutes enjoying your vacation. Then very slowly count to ten. You have returned from your vacation. Slowly raise your body, and open your eyes.

Talk about how each of you felt during this exercise. It is normal for several people to have different reactions.

Assertiveness

Case 1: You've been on a successful weight loss program for two weeks. You're at a party and someone keeps trying to get you to eat a piece of cake. You've told the person, "No, thank you," but she keeps coming back and bothering you. What do you do?

Case 2: You're at a football game with a girlfriend. Two teenage boys, whom neither of you know, come over and sit next to you. They try talking with you and are obviously trying to pick you both up. You and your friend have no interest in either of them. What do you do?

Both situations call for you to be assertive. Assertiveness means expressing your feelings, ideas, and beliefs in an honest and direct manner without violating another person's rights. Assertiveness is *not* aggression. Aggression violates the rights of others and usually is hostile and attacking. You can be assertive without being aggressive.

In Case 1, an assertive response could be: "I'm trying to lose weight. I would appreciate it if you would not ask me again about the cake," said in a firm but pleasant voice.

In Case 1, an aggressive response would be: "Look, get that cake out of my face or I'll make you eat it all!" said in a loud, nasty tone.

In Case 2, an assertive response would be: "My friend and I are enjoying the game and would prefer to watch it by ourselves."

In Case 2, an aggressive response would be: "You're not my type. Get lost."

In Case 1, someone who was not assertive might have left the party in order to escape the persistent cake person, or she may have eaten the cake just so the person wouldn't keep asking her. In Case 2, the nonassertive person might have left the game or let the boys sit with her even through she did not want their company. These actions avoid the real issues as well as violate the true needs of the nonassertive person.

How can you be more assertive? Try some of these activities:

- Watch other people who you think are assertive. Try to model your behavior after theirs.
- Pay attention to the times when you are not assertive and when you are assertive. In what types of situations is it hardest for you to be assertive? Work on those particular situations.
- Imagine yourself being assertive or think about an instance when you were assertive. Think about how good you feel when you stand up for your rights.
- Act out being assertive by role-playing with friends.
- Practice in everyday life situations. The more you practice, the easier it gets.

Get together with some friends and design a set of skits showing assertive, aggressive, and nonassertive behavior. Put on these skits for others. These are some situations you can use.

- Someone is playing very loud music in a nearby apartment.
- The smoke from someone's cigarette is going in your face.
- Someone gets a well-done hamburger, when she ordered it medium-rare.
- Someone buys a "super-duper" waterproof backpack that she finds out later is not waterproof at all.
- Someone is standing in line at the movie theater and another person cuts in front of her.

Remember that your assertive response will not always get you what you want (for instance, the store may refuse to refund your money for the defective product you purchased). However, you will still benefit from being assertive—it feels good to stand up for yourself!

Personal Safety

Ever since you were a child, you've probably learned many ways to protect yourself. Stay away from strangers; never hitchhike; don't walk home alone at night; report any suspicious or strange-looking person. All these safety rules are important to know, but staying safe is a lot harder than watching out for the crazy-looking stranger. Statistics show that most often young people are harmed or abused by someone they know and trust. It's important to know how to avoid potentially dangerous situations at home, at school, in public places, on the street, on dates, and when babysitting. It's equally important to know how to say no to someone who tries to harm you or force you to do anything against your will—something that's especially hard to do when you feel threatened or if you know the person.

Let's take a look at the experiences of several girls and see how they handled some of these situations. Discuss what you would have done. Then, review the safety tips.

Toni

After an evening of shopping, Toni and Candy decided that they would part company in the last hour before the stores in the mall closed and would meet at the main entrance at 9:30 P.M. On her way to Proctor's Shoe Store, Toni noticed uneasily that one particular man with curly red hair always seemed to be around as she walked along. Yet the man was well dressed and didn't appear sinister. Toni put it out of her mind as she turned into Proctor's. She managed to select a pair of shoes and pay just before closing time. She then set out to meet Candy back at the other end of the mall. Strolling past the now closed shops, she felt a surge of fear when she spotted the red-haired man walking behind her. The mall was rapidly becoming deserted and Toni was beginning to feel panicky. What are Toni's options? What could she have done earlier to avoid her present predicament?

One of the most important safety tips to remember is to avoid placing yourself in a potentially dangerous situation. Candy and Toni shouldn't have separated at a time when they might well be alone in the mall. Toni should have paid attention to her first fears. Looks are not a good basis for determining good or bad intentions. Toni could have told someone in the shoe store about her worries. Even now, Toni can still protect herself by walking quickly or even running to another person in the mall. And if she really feels threatened, she shouldn't feel embarrassed about screaming for help.

Gayle

When the father of the child Gayle was babysitting for came home drunk, he still insisted on driving her home. Gayle was afraid to be rude or hurt Mr. Anderson's feelings, so she did not object to his driving her home.

Gayle should have called her parents and requested that they pick her up or have her take a taxi home. Mr. Anderson was in no state to drive her home safely. Never let the risk of hurting someone's feelings make you take chances with your own life. Both Gayle and Mr. Anderson could have been injured or killed in a car accident.

Jan

Jan went on her second date with a boy from high school. The movie they went to see ended earlier than expected. On the way home, he said they might as well take the longer way home since they had more time. Jan didn't object until he pulled off into a parking area. When he began to pressure her to have sex, she refused. He became very angry and threatening, telling her that she had agreed to come this way so she was asking for it. Jan felt very frightened and gave in. Afterwards, she was extremely upset but was afraid to tell anyone what had happened.

Jan was the victim of an acquaintance rape, since she was forced to have sex by someone she knew. If you are threatened with a sexual attack, stay calm, don't panic. Panic makes it impossible for you to think rationally enough to do the following important things:

- Look for an avenue of escape.
- Try to talk your way out of the situation.
- Do not be pressured by guilt or statements that you agreed to do it.
- Determine if it is safe to physically resist.
- If others are near enough to hear, scream and shout "fire!" or call out for someone to call the police.

After any incident:

- Remember, it is not your fault.
- Tell an adult whom you trust.
- Report the rape to the police. Forced sex, even when committed by someone you agreed to date, is a serious crime.

Kristy

Note: A situation may arise where you become concerned about the personal safety of a friend or relative. Sometimes you can play an important role in safeguarding the well-being of others. You may even have the opportunity to save a life.

Kristy knew that Deanna had been feeling more and more unhappy. It seemed that Deanna was dissatisfied with just about everything—family, friends, and school. She was becoming more moody and withdrawn. Kristy noticed that many of the friends and activities that had brought them so much enjoyment seemed no longer to mean anything to Deanna. Kristy felt that once summer vacation began, she could coax her friend out of her depression, but lately she was wondering whether Deanna's mood might be really serious. Some of Deanna's comments frightened her, especially when Deanna said that "everything might be better if it were just all over."

What can and should Kristy do? She is right to be afraid for her friend. She is getting signals that the situation may be very serious. Deanna might even be contemplating suicide. Many times friends are often the first to recognize that things are getting out of hand. Kristy should seek help for her friend. Family members, teachers, guidance counselors, health professionals, crisis intervention centers, members of the clergy, all can help. Often a potential suicide victim is

72

indirectly asking for help when she or he gives clues about feelings of despair and suicidal thoughts. Kristy's concern and follow-up might save a life.

Brenda

Brenda had noticed for two days that her neighbor was staring at her as she passed his house on the way home from school. On the third day, he stopped her and invited her in for a chat. Since he was a friend of the family, she accepted his offer. Partway through the conversation, he leaned very close and he touched her breast. When Brenda pulled back very startled, he told her it was an accident and then told her not to tell anyone.

If Brenda was suspicious of her neighbor's behavior, she should have refused to enter his home. Once he started to touch her, Brenda should have forcefully said no and run out of his house. Brenda should *not* keep this a secret, but should tell an adult she trusts. No one has a right to touch you or force themselves on you in any way. Never feel guilty or somehow to blame.

Joan

Joan was feeling no worries about driving because she had had her license for over five months now and was good at handling the family car. She was, however, worried about getting to band practice late. Her friends Donna and Audrey jumped quickly into the car, not bothering with seat belts. On the two-lane road that led to the school, Jan fumed as she motored along slowly behind a truck that was doing just below the speed limit. Donna urged Joan to pass the truck and speed up. Feeling pressured, Joan began tailgating and then swung out in the oncoming lane to pass. It was then that she saw the red van. Swerving to avoid a collision, she lost control and ran off the road into a ditch. When Joan came to, Donna was unconscious and her head was bleeding and Audrey, who had been in the back seat, was thrown into the front of the car.

Car accidents are the major cause of death and serious injury among teenagers. Many times, accidents occur not because of the basic incapability of the driver but because of driving conditions or failures of judgment. Seat belts help to prevent injury and death. Joan, Donna, and Audrey should not have neglected to use seat belts because they were in a rush. Legally, Joan as the driver is responsible for the accident, even though Donna urged her to speed up and pass.

In each of the above cases, the girl was placed in a potentially harmful or dangerous situation. To protect yourself, you should think in advance about what you would do. This will help you to avoid panicking if the situation should occur.

OTHER PERSONAL SAFETY ACTIVITIES

■ Think of a place or situation (for example, at home, on a date, baby-sitting, or in the street) and prepare a list of relevant personal safety tips for younger girls.

■ Try several of the activities in the Contemporary Issues booklet *Staying Safe*, a GSUSA publication.

■ Take an American Red Cross first aid course or equivalent. Have on hand a book giving current safety and first aid information, such as *Standard First Aid and Personal Safety*.

Looking Ahead

Make a daily commitment to follow a healthy lifestyle. Remember, you're in charge of your own well-being!

Your future is filled with endless possibilities. As you learn more about yourself and develop the unique qualities and talents you have, you can look ahead to a full, rewarding life.

Making Decisions

Every day you make hundreds of decisions—what time to wake up in the morning, what to eat for breakfast, what to wear, what to write on a test, whether you should participate in a discussion in class, etc., etc., etc. Many decisions are almost automatic—habits carried on without much thinking. However, sometimes you have to make a decision about something that is important to you (perhaps it's deciding which interest project to work on, what to do to make yourself more attractive, whether you should go to college). At those times, going through the following decision-making steps may be helpful to you:

1. Figure out what the *real* issue is. Identify the problem that requires a decision. Is the issue: What college should I attend? Or is the issue: Should I go to college?
2. Obtain whatever information you will need to arrive at a decision. Think about your feelings, values, goals, and interests as well as the effect of your decision on other people.
3. Think of all the possible decisions you could make. Writing a list is often helpful.
4. Evaluate each possible decision. Look at both the positive and negative aspects of each decision. Each point should not necessarily carry the same weight in your decision-making. For example, a very large negative (my best friend will never speak to me again) should carry more weight than a small positive (it will be fun for a couple of hours).
5. Make a decision after you've considered all the information you have.
6. Carry out your decision. Start working on the interest project or fitness plan you selected. Start filling out the job or college application form.
7. From time to time, reevaluate your decision. As you and your circumstances change, you may need to start the decision-making process over again. A different decision may need to be made.

REACHING YOUR GOALS

Once you've made the decision to do something—exercise more, get a higher grade in a subject you have not been doing well in, put your photos into an album, rearrange your room—you'll need a plan to make it happen.

Try to achieve your goal by following these steps:

1. Identify a specific goal that can reasonably be accomplished in one or two months (for example, a B average instead of a C).
2. For one week, don't do anything special; just *monitor* your behavior in the selected area. Keeping a written record helps. For instance, if your goal is to exercise more, write down all the kinds of physical activities you do. Keep track also of times you could be more active (for example, walking instead of waiting for a ride). You may have more opportunities to exercise than you thought you did.
3. Review the record of your behavior during the one-week self-monitoring period. Use what you learn to develop a specific plan to reach your goal. For instance, if you find that you usually spend an hour one night a week talking on the phone, see whether you and your friend could get together for an aerobics class instead.
4. Think of ways to reward yourself (for instance, going somewhere special) for getting closer to your goal and then reward yourself as you *do* get closer.
5. If you have been successful in reaching your first goal, you might want to identify and work toward a second goal.

If you have not been able to reach your goal, try to figure out what happened. Were you striving for an unrealistic goal (going from a C average to an A in just one month)? Were you not motivated enough to accomplish your goal? (Perhaps the interest project you selected was not as interesting as you thought it would be.) Was your goal not important enough for you to apply a great deal of effort? (Think about how important it really is for you to put the photos you've saved for five years into an album.)

If you are still interested in pursuing your goal, revise your plan and get started again!

Money Management

By the time you reach Cadette and Senior Girl Scouting, you have been using money for some time. However, learning to *manage* money is a skill that can be developed over a lifetime! In today's world it is very important to be educated about finances—especially your own.

One way to find out how you can handle your money is to keep a record of it. For one month, keep track of every cent you receive and every cent you spend. When the month's totals are in, review them. What percentage of your income (money coming in) came from an allowance? What percentage was earned? What did you spend your money on? How much did you save?

BUDGETING

After you analyze how you handle money, make a budget for a month. A budget is a financial plan that helps people organize their money management.

Your personal monthly budget could look something like this:

Monthly Budget

Income

	Estimated	Actual
1. Allowance	$_____	_____
2. Earnings	_____	_____
3. Other income (gifts, bank interest on savings, etc.)	_____	_____
TOTAL INCOME	$_____	$_____

(To get your total income, add lines 1, 2, and 3.)

Fixed expenses
(expenses that usually stay the same)

	Estimated	Actual
Transportation	$_____	_____
Troop dues	_____	_____
Other	_____	_____
TOTAL FIXED EXPENSES	$_____	$_____

Flexible expenses
(expenses that vary from day to day)

	Estimated	Actual
Food	$_____	_____
Clothing	_____	_____
Gifts and donations to charities	_____	_____
Entertainment	_____	_____
Other	_____	_____
TOTAL FLEXIBLE EXPENSES	$_____	$_____

Savings

	Estimated	Actual
	$_____	$_____
TOTAL OF EXPENSES AND SAVINGS	$_____	$_____

After you estimate what your expenses will be and have filled in the estimated amounts of all your fixed and flexible expenses and the amount you hope to save, subtract those totals from your total income. If you get a negative number, you're planning to spend or save too much! You will have to make some choices. Following the suggestions in the decision-making section on pages 74–75 may help you. Strive for a balanced budget with expenses and savings equal to income.

Try your budget out for one month. Keep a record of how much you actually are spending and how much your actual income is for the month. Look at your results. Was your budget accurate? Make any budget revisions you feel are necessary and try it out again for another month.

BANKING

You may already be familiar with banks and the services they provide to their customers. To learn more, get first-hand information from a banker about the banking procedures in your community—checking accounts, credit cards, savings accounts, mortgages, student loans, home improvement loans, consumer loans, and so forth. Throughout your life you will most likely be using several of the above-mentioned accounts.

Another way to find out about money management is to organize a series of "finance clinics." Invite other girls and boys your age to attend. Get the "experts" in your community to help—lawyers, insurance agents, stockbrokers, bankers. Just finding out who the experts are will be an education in itself. Any one of these subjects is important to know about and would make a good topic for a finance clinic: (1) advantages and disadvantages of cash buying and credit buying—charge accounts, short-term and long-term installment buying, credit cards, loans; (2) taxes—federal, state, and local—on income, sales, property; (3) investments—stocks, bonds, mutual funds.

CONSUMER AWARENESS

Another important aspect of personal money management is consumer awareness. Are you an educated consumer? How are you influenced by fads, trends, and advertising? Does television play a role in what you purchase and what you want to purchase? For one week, keep a list of everything you buy, how much each item costs, and your reason for buying it. When the week is over, look at your list. Think about the above questions and answer them for yourself. Find ways to learn more as a consumer. Read the newspaper, read labels on items you purchase, watch consumer awareness programs on television, and try the Money Management and Entrepreneurship interest projects.

Time Management

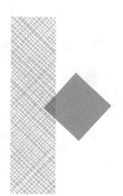

In this busy society of ours, it's important to be able to manage your time. Do you have time for yourself? for building relationships with others? for schoolwork? for other work? for recreation and hobbies? Is your life balanced?

One way to study how you're managing your time is to keep a time diary. In your diary, keep track of what you do and the time spent doing it for one week. Then look through it and see how your time was managed. Is a lot of your time spent in one area to the exclusion of others? Do you waste a lot of time? How could you have improved the way you managed your time during the week?

If you seem to have trouble with time management, try experimenting with the way you use your time. Try things at different times. If you always do your homework directly after school, try doing something else after school and doing your homework later in the evening. If you always do your exercises only at night, try doing them sometimes in the morning. See what happens, see how you feel. Sometimes it's helpful to experiment with time because you may find new and better ways to organize your life. It's easy to get into a routine that isn't working well for you. In such a case, it helps to be flexible and try something else.

Some other helpful hints about time management include the following:

■ When you have a lot to do, *do the important things first*. Then you can go on to the other tasks—do them in order of your priorities.

■ *Find your work pace*. Everyone works at a different pace, some slowly, some in fast bursts of energy. Find what works best for you.

■ *Finish tasks*. Try to finish most of what you start (but don't feel you must complete something that no longer has any value for you).

■ *Concentrate*. Things that are done when you concentrate are usually done more thoroughly, skillfully, and effectively than tasks that are done when you are distracted and unfocused. Find the way that you concentrate best—in a room alone with the door closed; in a library where other people are around; while listening to music.

■ *Take breaks*. Avoid "burn-out." Know when to stop. Refresh yourself, rest, eat, exercise, or do something else for a while.

■ *Avoid clutter*. Clutter can literally mess things up! It can slow you down if you constantly have to hunt to find things. Organize your surroundings so they work for you.

■ *Don't delay*. Many people keep putting things off until they face a real time crunch. Don't procrastinate.

■ *Avoid perfectionism*. Many times it's more important to get things done than to wait to do them perfectly. It's important to do as good a job as you can, but don't fall into the trap of failing to complete something because of perfectionism.

■ *Delegate tasks*. Many people feel they have to do everything themselves and often exhaust themselves needlessly. Tasks can be more fun and may be accomplished more quickly and effectively when they are shared and delegated.

■ *Simplify*. When you're feeling overwhelmed by everything you think you need to do, simplify your life as much as possible. Sometimes you may need to say "no" to tasks and requests and follow some of the time management hints above.

Hobbies

Some people develop their interests through their hobbies. A hobby is any type of activity one does during leisure time for relaxation, for pleasure, to learn something new, or to develop a skill.

Do you have a hobby? Do you have interests that can be turned into a hobby? For example, a love of horses could become a collecting hobby where you collect horse figures and photographs, or perhaps you could study equestrian skills.

Do the activity described below to learn more about your interests:

If you could have five gifts, which of the following would you choose? Select one from each column.

A	B	C	D	E
Trip to a foreign country	Microscope	Concert tickets	Chemistry set	Subscription to a sports magazine
Horse	Camera	Encyclopedia	Oil paints	Magnifying glass
Trip to the Olympics	Music lessons	Hiking boots	Model car kit	Rock collection
Computer	Tent	Binoculars	Plant collection	Shell collection
Car	Scuba diving outfit	Record collection	Tool kit	Field guide
Rafting expedition	Skiis	Backpack	Gardening tools	Cookbook
	Library of novels	Warm-up suit	Jewelry-making kit	Basketball
	Gold bracelet	Tickets to a tennis match	Macramé set	Sweater
	Pet dog	New outfit for school	Board game	
	Sewing machine		Skating lessons	
	Aquarium			

What do your selections tell you about your interests?

Ask some friend or family members to do this activity. Compare your answers with theirs.

STARTING A HOBBY

To start a hobby, do some research. Go to the library and look through books and magazines that deal with it. You can also try to find someone who has the same hobby you're interested in. Ask that person to share information with you. Or join a club that is practicing that hobby.

Your values, interests, and hobbies may lead you to a career. Many artists began as children with art hobbies. Many athletes began with games and sports hobbies. Considering the values, interests, and hobbies you have now, in what types of careers do you see yourself? Fill out the chart below and see the "From Dreams to Reality: Career Exploration" chapter. You may have very strong feelings and ideas about what you might or might not want to do. The important thing is to work on getting to know yourself and what you really want, remembering that your needs and interests change throughout your life.

Values Examples:	Interests	Hobbies	Possible Careers
Healthy living	Food, nutrition	Cooking	Nutritionist, chef, caterer, restaurateur, food writer, researcher, product demonstrator
Conservation of the natural environment	Animals, plants	Observing wildlife, nature photography	Wildlife biologist, teacher, ranger, botanist, zoologist, veterinarian
_____	_____	_____	_____
_____	_____	_____	_____
_____	_____	_____	_____

This chapter has charted a small portion of the skills you'll need throughout your life. There are also a number of interest projects that can help you develop greater expertise and increase the scope of these skills. See *Cadette and Senior Girl Scout Interest Projects* for the full range of possibilities. Every day will add new experiences that will increase your repertory of life skills. Learning should never stop. That way, with every twist or turn your future path takes, you will be better able to anticipate the best move, turn adversity into opportunity, and be in control of your life.

6

FROM DREAMS TO REALITY: CAREER EXPLORATION

ork will be a part of your entire life. Every job you ever hold—whether as an employee, a volunteer, or in a home setting—is a part of your life's career. Career planning isn't like a mathematical problem that has one right answer. Career planning is a lifelong process and, at different stages of your life as your career opportunities, options, and dilemmas change, so too will your choices, decisions, and solutions. In a sense, you are involved in a career right now. Attending school, doing homework, and having household responsibilities all involve work responsibilities and decision-making. So do other types of jobs you may have, such as babysitting, tutoring others, or having a paper route.

When you enjoy your work, and are interested in and challenged by your

career, you are doing something positive for your self-esteem. It is crucial for you to make your own choices about your future. If you drift into a way of life because you didn't make decisions, you may find yourself out of control of your own life.

It is important that you receive the best available vocational and educational training you can, and that you think of yourself as someone with a lifelong career. The thought of being in control of your life's work will encourage you to set your own goals and priorities. That means taking charge of your life and accepting decision-making responsibilities (see pages 74–75).

In this chapter you will explore traditional and nontraditional careers, learn job-seeking skills, see what networking is all about, enjoy role-playing and other career exploration games, explode myths about women and work, glimpse into the future, and fantasize. Hopefully you will envision your future as being full of possibilities you never before imagined!

It's Up to You

To discover your career interests, try testing yourself against various possibilities. Here is a fun way to do it. In each of the following pairs, circle the one you'd prefer to do. Be sure to circle the code letters too. They will be explained later.

WB feed a sick child
OD feed a tiger

OD throw a ball
  A throw a piece of pottery on a
         potter's wheel

  A hook a rug
 TT hook up a stereo system

OD go hiking
  A go caroling

  P plan a political campaign
  A plan a movie

  A take a picture
 WB take a person's temperature

 TT ride a spaceship
  A ride a movie boom

  A design a dress
 WB design a health and fitness trail

OD plan an overnight camping trip
  P plan a gathering for
        international students

 TT study the business page in the
        newspaper
OD study wildlife conservation

  P research a genealogy
  A research a novel

OD operate a fish hatchery
  P operate a computer

OD learn to ski
  P learn to speak a foreign
        language

A write a story			**TT** work in a laboratory	
WB write a health tips newsletter			**WB** work in a school	

P give advice to a school dropout
TT give advice to a business owner

OD discover a mountain pass
TT discover a new medicine

WB help care for a sick child
P help a lonely child learn a game

TT study accounting
P study sociology

WB hold a meeting for social workers
TT hold a meeting for deep-sea explorers

WB visit a nursery school
TT visit a computer facility

WB carry a stethoscope
OD carry a basketball

A peer through a camera lens
TT peer through a microscope

OD climb a mountain
P climb an archaelogical site

WB counsel a peer who is suicidal
P counsel a person planning foreign travel

TT talk to a surgeon
OD talk to a zookeeper

A set a gem
WB set a broken bone

WB visit a hospital
A visit a play rehearsal

TT do an experiment
WB do an exercise routine

OD read a map
A read a short story

OD make a bird feeder
P make a toy

P choose a country to visit
OD choose a sport to play

A tour an art museum
P tour an historical building

P give a party
TT give a speech

OD cast a mold of an animal track
A cast a wax mold for a silver pendant

Count the letters you have circled and place the totals in the boxes here. How many of each are there?

_____ **WB**   _____ **P**   _____ **TT**   _____ **A**   _____ **OD**

These letters give you hints about your interests and abilities. Here's what they mean:

WB Well-Being careers appeal to you. You're concerned. You want to care for others' physical and emotional needs.

P People careers interest you. You enjoy meeting new people. You like solving problems with people and for people.

TT Today and Tomorrow careers are for you. You're science- and business-oriented. You're inquisitive, and finding out about the hows and whys of things appeals to you.

A Arts careers are for you. You're creative. You like performing, communicating, and/or making beautiful objects.

OD Out-of-Doors careers appeal to you. You're active, adventurous, and you like sports and nature.

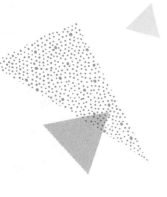

How did you choose? How do you feel about what your choices tell you? Remember that this is a very simple measure of your interests. Your school guidance counselor will know of more accurate interest inventories you might take.

You've Got What It Takes

Different careers call for different abilities. Some jobs may require you to concentrate, some may require you to communicate; most will require a combination of many abilities. What are your abilities and how do they relate to different careers?

Look at the list of abilities on the chart that follows. Remember, this chart is only a beginning tool and far from complete. Can you add to this list?

Place a check mark in the left-hand column next to each ability that *you* have. In deciding which items to check, you might want to consider your strong points and accomplishments. Also, an honest conversation with a person who knows you well may reveal abilities you never dreamed you had.

Now, choose any five careers that are presently of interest to you. If you are undecided, use the information from the previous activity to help you make a decision. Write the career titles in the spaces provided at the top of the chart. Place a check mark next to each ability you think is needed for the careers you have listed.

You	Abilities	Careers				
_____	Intellectual	_____	_____	_____	_____	_____
_____	Scientific	_____	_____	_____	_____	_____
_____	Artistic	_____	_____	_____	_____	_____
_____	Physical	_____	_____	_____	_____	_____
_____	Athletic	_____	_____	_____	_____	_____
_____	Manual	_____	_____	_____	_____	_____
_____	Clerical	_____	_____	_____	_____	_____
_____	Musical	_____	_____	_____	_____	_____
_____	Creative	_____	_____	_____	_____	_____
_____	Organizational	_____	_____	_____	_____	_____
_____	Persuasive	_____	_____	_____	_____	_____
_____	Social	_____	_____	_____	_____	_____
_____	Outgoing	_____	_____	_____	_____	_____
_____	Verbal	_____	_____	_____	_____	_____
_____	Mathematical	_____	_____	_____	_____	_____
_____	Analytical	_____	_____	_____	_____	_____

Compare the "you" column to the career columns you have completed. Do they match? If there are differences, what can you do to acquire the abilities you are lacking? You might want to share the results of this activity with your group leader, your family, a guidance counselor, or a close friend. These people may provide additional insights for you to think about.

Suggestion: You can redo this chart on separate paper to include as many careers and abilities as you wish.

The Work Setting

An important career consideration is the work environment. Some people prefer working indoors, others like the outdoors, and still others want a combination. Many people enjoy a busy atmosphere and the chance for a lot of interaction with people; others seek complete solitude. Think carefully about your ideal work environment. Will it include any of the following elements?

telephone	grass	fluorescent lights	noise
car	books	enclosed office	paintings
outdoors	animals	typewriter	sunshine
water	moonlight	machines	people
plants	tools	desk	

Using these items as a starting point, imagine your ideal work environment. Make a list of everything you would like it to include.

With your list as a guide, thumb through an old magazine for scenes or items that fit into your ideal job setting. What kinds of careers are possible in the work setting you most prefer? How can careers be adapted to fit an ideal work setting, or the setting adapted to the career?

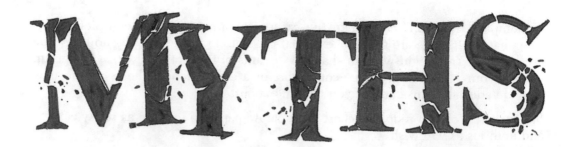

Exploding Myths

Myths are sometimes created to explain what people don't understand. The following myths concerning work are "exploded" here for you:

Myth #1:

What you learn in high school has little to do with what you need to know in your career.

Exploded: The skills acquired in high school lay the foundation for many of your future educational pursuits. The courses you don't take can affect your career plans as much as the subjects you do take. Also, good study habits and self-discipline in high school prepare you for the challenges of the work world.

Myth #2:

If you don't go to college, you won't get a good job.

Exploded: A college education is only one of several options in preparing for future careers. The Bureau of Labor Statistics predicts that there will be increased job opportunities for highly skilled workers such as plumbers and carpenters. The only certainty about the work world is that there are no guarantees for anyone, college-educated or not.

Myth #3:

Women don't have to worry about planning a career because they end up with marriage and children.

Exploded: More than half of the women who are married and living with their husbands are in the paid labor force. Most women with children between six and 18 years old are working outside the home. More than half of all women 16 years or older are workers. Many women choose to remain single.

Myth #4:

Sexism does not exist anymore.

Exploded: Almost 80 percent of women workers are concentrated in low-paying jobs with little hope of advancement. As a result, the average woman worker earns about three-fifths of what a man earns, even when both work full-time year-round.

Myth #5:

There is one appropriate career track for each person.

Exploded: According to the U.S. Department of Labor, people change careers at an average of three to five times during their lifetime. The old custom of holding one career per lifetime has faded. For example, a person who started as a junior high school teacher may enter politics and eventually leave public office to become a professor of political science.

You may choose a career and remain in it, decide to exchange it for another career, or combine it with a different career. Just be aware that you have many choices at any stage of your life. Don't allow these myths and others to become self-fulfilling prophecies—to come true because you believe they are true.

Exploring Careers

Imagine that you are 40 years old. A movie has just been made on the story of your life and you are about to see it. The theater darkens; the reel spins; the movie begins. What is the title? Who are the important people in your life? Where do you live? Where do you work? What are your accomplishments? What type of life are you living? Write your fantasy as a story, poem, play, or journal entry. Use pictures or drawings if you wish to illustrate it.

Exploring careers can be an exciting adventure. As you acquaint yourself with a variety of careers, you will have a larger knowledge base to draw upon when you need to set your own career goals.

The following random list includes careers you may know little if anything about. Some are jobs in the trades that often involve manual labor; others are office jobs that often require college degrees; still others require a combination of skills and training.

X-ray technician	dietician	referee/umpire	camp director
physical therapist	musician	tour guide	postal worker
wardrobe consultant	illustrator	stockbroker	dentist
writer	statistician	research scientist	cinematographer
caterer	lithographer	politician	speech writer
plumber	chef	judge	press secretary
physician	hairdresser	personnel officer	salesperson
architect	farmer	chemist	electrician
pilot	athletic coach	fashion designer	investment banker
auto mechanic	psychologist	engineer	speech pathologist
broadcaster	teacher	librarian	accountant ✓
telephone repairer	child care worker	school principal	surveyor
financial analyst	police officer	editor	jeweler
publicity agent	computer programmer	cosmetologist	nurse
interior designer	attorney ✓	photographer	painter
carpenter	lobbyist	bus driver	veterinarian
college professor	marketing researcher	animal breeder	paralegal
butcher	social worker	landscaper	actor
anesthetist	stunt person	ecologist	forest ranger

Select three careers. At least one of them should be a career you are interested in, and one should be a career about which you know little but are curious to learn more. Working alone or with a partner, use a variety of resources to find out as much as you can about each career: library, people working in that field, businesses, the U.S. Department of Labor, and so on. Turn one of your troop or group meetings into a career information night, and take turns discussing your findings. You may want to invite guest speakers to offer additional information.

KNOW WHAT TO LOOK FOR

Your information hunt should include the following:

1. *Job description*. What do workers really do? How do they fill their days? What skills do they have? What machines or materials do they use? What clothing or uniforms are required?

2. *Education or training.* What credentials are needed to hold the job? Would the job allow you to earn money while working toward necessary credentials or while serving an apprenticeship?

3. *Pay and benefits.* What is the pay range? Are workers paid hourly or given an annual salary? Are commissions included in the pay package? What are the fringe benefits (sick leave, medical insurance, vacation time, etc.)?

4. *Advantages.* What are some of the hidden benefits? Will you get to travel, set your own hours, be given a car, or . . . ?

5. *Disadvantages.* What are some of the less pleasant aspects of the job? Are there occupational hazards? Is the job steady, seasonal, or with many strikes and layoffs, or . . . ?

6. *Personal benefits.* What do workers consider to be the personal rewards of the job? What are the opportunities for advancement?

Career Creation

In choosing a career, you'll need to consider many things: your interests, your talents and abilities, the setting in which you want to work, the amount of education you are willing to commit yourself to, your salary requirement, and the sort of clothing you'll feel most comfortable in on the job. The question is, can you find an ideal job—one that realistically combines all of your preferences? To help you answer this question, try out some sample combinations in a group of five people.

Each group member rolls a die. Match the number that appears with the information on the following chart and record your results on a piece of paper. For example, the first toss determines the amount of education required. If you roll a three, look at the third line in the education column and you see that the job requires two years of college. The second toss determines whether the job deals with people, numbers, beauty and art, physical activity, technology, or the environment. Toss three indicates work setting. The fourth toss determines the clothing suitable for the job, and toss five reveals salary range.

First Toss Education/Training	Second Toss Interest	Third Toss Setting	Fourth Toss Clothing	Fifth Toss Salary
1. High school education	People	Office	Suit or dress	$0–$15,000
2. Training beyond high school	Numbers	Outdoors	Skirt and blouse	$15,000–$25,000
3. Two years of college	Beauty and art	Mobile (traveling from place to place)	Uniform	$25,000–$35,000
4. Four years of college	Physical activity	Hospital	Jeans and T-shirt	$35,000–$45,000
5. Two years of graduate school	Technology	School/ university	Pants and top	$45,000–$55,000
6. More than two years of professional/ graduate school	Environment	Studio	Lab coat/smock	Over $55,000

After five tosses, your group will have recorded five different aspects of a job. Now select a career from the list on page 88 that meets all of these requirements.

Consider this combination: four years of college, $15,000–$25,000, physical activity, outdoors, uniform. An athletic coach fits this description. Can you think of anyone else?

Of course, your five tosses may indicate an unlikely combination: for example, high school education, over $55,000, environment, office, uniform. For a combination like this one, your group may not find a matching career. In this case, discuss what makes the combination unrealistic. What one requirement would you substitute to make the career profile more realistic?

A Job vs. a Career

"It's just a job." "I have a career." What makes the difference between a job and a career?

You!

If your work:

- is something you have to do
- doesn't particularly fit into your long-term plans
- is boring

The job market controls you!

If your work:

- is in a career position that utilizes your talents, interests, and background preparation
- lets you feel in charge
- fits into your long-term career goals
- interests you
- is something you want to do and enjoy doing

You have career control!

To start on the road to career control, it's important to think and plan. Think about your

- likes and dislikes
- interests
- strengths and weaknesses
- talents and abilities
- opportunities and obstacles
- preferred work setting
- salary requirement
- willingness to obtain the necessary education
- preferences regarding clothing on the job

Careers Unlimited

A woman's place is in a research lab, on a tractor, in a classroom, in space, in the news, in electronics, in sales, on the Supreme Court, underwater, in an operating room . . . .

The history of women in the work world is long and varied. Throughout the past 300 years, American women have worked, contributed to society, and dealt with changing life situations. They often worked in nontraditional jobs (those in which about 75 percent of the people in the field are men), especially when they were single or widowed or during times of war. So, your female forebears were always *able* to do "men's work"; they just weren't always *allowed* to. Many positions are more commonly held by men than women, yet offer women the opportunity to earn higher salaries. (Note: Men working in jobs that are nontraditional for them often earn more than the women in those same fields.) Many of these jobs require specialized skills that women can readily learn, and as trainees they can earn while they learn. In some cases, there may be a variety of schedules or shifts to choose from, usually with higher pay for overtime and night work.

Make a list of job positions that you don't usually associate with women. Find out about those jobs. Also see if you can find out about any women who hold these jobs. Try to learn more about them and the work they do.

- From the list of careers on page 88, identify those that are not commonly held by women.
- Add other examples of nontraditional jobs and roles for women.
- Hold a "careers unlimited" forum. You could do this for a group of younger girls. Collect brochures, prepare informational fliers, prepare displays about all the different careers that women can pursue.
- Interview local women in nontraditional careers. See what they have to say about their work and about women entering that field.

Traditionally girls have had fewer career options than boys, and even now that more fields are open to them, most young women still limit their choices to traditional careers.

IT'S A WOMAN'S WORLD

As a group, brainstorm a list of jobs that have been traditionally held by males or by females. Then think of a dilemma that a person of the opposite sex would face if she/he applied for or held that job. Here are a couple of ideas to start you off:

- Visitors come to your office wishing to see the vice president of the company. They ask to see your boss, before they learn that you are the vice president.
- A woman applies for a job as: a telephone installer, an athletic coach, an electrician, a bank president, a chief of police.

In small groups, select a situation to role-play. Afterwards, discuss the situations you acted out. How did each person feel when caught in her situation? Is there more than one effective solution to each dilemma?

Further Career Exploration Activities

FASHION FAIR

A job may require clothing such as a suit or dress or a more casual outfit such as jeans and a flannel shirt. Some jobs require that a uniform be worn at work each day. Whatever the requirements, it is important that you adapt comfortably to the dress code needed to do your job effectively.

Put your fashion sense to work to select a career wardrobe. Choose two careers that interest you (look at the career list on page 88 for some ideas). Then put together a wardrobe for these two careers plus a wardrobe for your free time.

Look through old magazines, newspapers, or pattern books. For each career, choose five ideal outfits—one for each day of the workweek. Be sure to consider coats, shoes, handbags, jewelry, and any other accessories you may want. And remember, money is no object.

When selecting each wardrobe, be sure to consider:

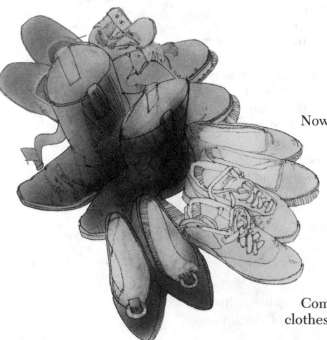

- The amount of physical activity the job requires
- The nature of any equipment that is needed—tools, machinery, motor vehicles, etc.
- The weather conditions (for outdoor jobs or jobs requiring travel)
- The people you will be dealing with

Now look closely at the wardrobes you have selected.

- What is the basic look of each wardrobe?
- Do these outfits have anything in common?
- Are they formal or casual?
- Are they suitable for physical activity?
- Do they require expensive, complicated care or simple cleaning techniques?
- Which of the three wardrobe groupings is most appealing to you?

Compare your career wardrobe selections with the clothes you usually most like to wear.

DILEMMAS

Because of the fast pace of contemporary life and the variety of responsibilities in diverse areas—career, home, family, education/training, and community—people today seem to be faced with even more decisions than in the past. Decision-making is not just for special occasions. Every day you must make decisions that will in some way affect your life and your relationships. Many choices that you make today tend to influence your future.

Below is a brief sketch of a woman who is faced with a dilemma. Her situation calls for decision-making. Can you help her make an effective decision?

Cecilia grew up in an urban area. She studied economics in college and is currently employed in the international finance department of a bank. Her interests include music, writing, and travel. Lately she has also been developing quite an interest in photography. Her boyfriend owns a small printing business and is very active in the community. Cecilia's sister works for an airline and keeps in frequent touch even though she lives in another city.

Dilemma: Cecilia has just lost her job because of staff reductions in her department.

In a small group, see if you can brainstorm ideas on ways to resolve Cecilia's dilemma. Think about networking, combining skills in new and different patterns, different ways to put talents into action. Talk about the pros and cons of all the alternatives.

Think of other situations that present dilemmas. Try to use situations where a number of alternatives are possible.

THE NEXT STEP

Keep in mind that career choices do not have to last a lifetime. You will do as much choosing throughout your working life as you did when you selected your very first job. Often, it is only after you have made a decision that you realize its significance and impact on your life. To explore career decision-making, try this activity.

Here are partial histories of two women who have already made many career decisions in their lives. They must now make another one. In their current decisions, they will consider such factors as their background, family responsibilities, values, and personal resources. What would you recommend that each woman do?

Susan E.

1970 Enters high school. Plans for a career as an accountant.

1973 In junior year, enters special high school honors program in mathematics.

1974 Graduates and enters college.

1977 Meets Tim M.

1978 Graduates with B.S. degree in mathematics. Gets a job in an accounting firm.

1981   Marries Tim, who has a job as a manager in the lumber industry.

1983   Susan and Tim have a child. After a brief leave from her job, Susan begins to work part-time as a consultant.

1986   Susan returns to work full-time.

1987   Susan is ready to make a career change. She looks into banking and the computer science field.

Decision to Be Made

Return to school full-time to do graduate work.	Work part-time and go to school in the evenings part-time.	Find a job in the computer science field.	Take a salary cut to begin a career in banking.	Other (identify another possible career/life direction).

Araceli R.

1978   Enters high school. Develops talents and interest in art.

1981   In junior year, wins first place in statewide high school art competition.

1982   Graduates and enters art school.

1984   Is awarded a one-year fellowship to study art in Florence, Italy.

1985   Returns to United States. Exhibits art in several galleries throughout the state. Teaches Saturday art classes for children in a state-funded project and is a waitress part-time.

1986   Art begins to sell. Meets an agent who suggests that she move to New York, where there are more potential opportunities in the field.

Decision to Be Made

Try to get a grant from an arts institute to support herself while preparing for a one-woman exhibit.	Retrain for job as art therapist in a school for children with disabilities.	Move to New York. Try to find a job as a commercial artist.	Return to Europe to study.	Other (identify another possible career/life direction).

Would you have come up with the same career choices as Susan and Araceli did up to this point? Are there other possibilities? What factors should Susan and Araceli consider in making their decisions? What decisions would you recommend?

Share and discuss your decisions with others. In what ways do you agree? Disagree? Why?

JUGGLING JOBS

Imagine you are in your mid-thirties. You are married and have a four-month-old child. Now you need to return to full-time work. You find a job with hours from 9:00 to 5:00, five days a week, paying $20,000 a year. You must combine your roles as homemaker and parent with your full-time paying job. Your husband must share the household chores equitably with you.

In a small group, determine the daily household chores and activities that must be done by you and your husband on a typical working day. Your list should include at least the following items:

- Each must shower and dress.
- The dog must be walked three times a day.
- The baby must be fed breakfast.
- The baby must be dressed and brought to the baby-sitter's home.
- Each must travel to and from work.
- There must be clean laundry, especially baby clothes, for the next day.
- The baby must be picked up at the baby-sitter's.
- Dinner must be prepared and served.
- The baby must be fed dinner.
- The kitchen must be cleaned.
- The baby must be bathed and put to sleep.
- The home must be straightened up.
- The garbage must be taken out.

Decide who will do each chore, and how long each chore will take. (Don't forget to allow time for sleeping and time on the job.) Record the information on a chart.

Tally the hours on each person's chart and record the totals. In a 24-hour workday, how much time remains for this working couple? Does one person have more time than the other? Is the work evenly divided? How much time is there for the child (playing and teaching new skills)? How much time is there to do things as a couple? How much time is there to do things alone?

Ask a group of males in your age range to do this exercise. How do your results compare with theirs?

Have your group role-play what certain times of the day (such as 6:00–8:00 in the morning, or 5:00–7:00 in the evening) might be like for the working couple.

Suggestion: Think ahead. In ten years, will you be single? Will you be married? Will you have children? Will you have your own home to take care of? Will you be employed? How will you juggle all your responsibilities to work, home, family, friends?

Interview a variety of working women in your community. For instance, find out about the lifestyles of a single career woman, a divorced working woman with custody of her child, a married working woman with no children, a married career woman with a toddler and a teenage stepchild, a married career woman with school-age children.

How are each of these women managing their daily routines? Ask them if and how time and responsibilities are shared with others.

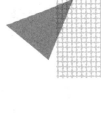

Lifestyles

The "traditional" family used to be a husband working outside the home and a wife at home taking care of two children under 18 years of age. Today, according to the Bureau of the Census, only 4 percent of all American households fit this pattern. In fact, only about 16 percent of the American population lives within a nuclear family (father, mother, and children). Women are heading families in increasing numbers, and women and their children make up the majority of those in poverty. Therefore, it appears wise to make long-range educational and career plans that will enable you to take financial responsibility for your life whether you are single or married.

The Future

There are many changes in life that can affect your career plans. Think about what you would do if the following occurred.

- The young man you are engaged to is suddenly transferred to another state and asks you to leave school.
- You have used up all the money for education you had, and are still undecided about your future career.
- You are pregnant but want to continue to work after your child is born.
- You have been offered a promotion, but it means moving to another state. Your husband enjoys his present job and is in a field where there are few openings.
- You have talent, training, and experience, but now can't find a job in your career field.
- You have worked for many years as a volunteer, but now you need to earn money.
- You inherit a family business, but you want to become a musician.

Hold a group session on these questions. Talk about what each of you would do in these different situations.

The Payoff

Careers come in all shapes and sizes. They also come in all price ranges. Some careers require more than ten years of study beyond college; others require a high school diploma or less. Some people feel that the extra years of study are not worth the effort, while others argue that the additional time and money spent preparing for a career are amply paid back when one considers the higher salary or greater satisfaction one can receive. What do you think? In order to come to a conclusion about this issue, you will need to know specific facts about probable incomes and career preparation costs.

Incomes are influenced by many factors, including the following:

1. Place of employment. (Urban areas, with their high cost of living, often—but not always—offer higher salaries.)
2. The amount of education and training you have.
3. The kind of education and training you have.
4. Whether you work for a profit or nonprofit organization or in the government.
5. Inflation. (The value of your income will decrease unless you receive raises equal to or greater than the inflation rate.)
6. Whether there is an oversupply or undersupply of people to fill a particular type of job.
7. Discriminatory practices. Although many laws have been passed to eliminate hiring practices that discriminate on the basis of age, sex, race, religion, or disabilities, there still are unfortunately many instances in which such discriminatory practices affect employment and income.
8. Whether you are represented by a union.

Career preparation costs are influenced by the following factors:

1. Whether you study at a public or private training facility, or public or private university. (Private costs are usually higher.)
2. Scholarships and grants you may receive.
3. Whether you complete your course work faster than generally expected.
4. Inflation, which frequently makes costs go up.

To get more specific information, consult:

■ People who have careers in which you are interested (always the best real-life information).
■ Career resource books.
■ Guidance counselors, career counselors.
■ Career information brochures and college bulletins from your school guidance office.
■ Books, pamphlets, and magazines from the library.
■ Organizations whose members are in the career you are studying.

Numbers/People/Things/Ideas

Most careers combine working with numbers, people, things (tools, equipment), and ideas. But each career combines them differently. The following activity shows how these concepts relate to various careers.

Look at the chart on the next page and decide how to rate each occupation that is listed. In the first example, people are of medium importance while numbers, things, and ideas are of high importance. Rate the rest of the occupations. Then add other occupations to the list and rate them. What are your interests and strengths? Which job may be best suited for you? Why?

| | Numbers | | | People | | | Things | | | Ideas | | |
	High	Medium	Low	High	Medium	Low	High	Medium	Low	High	Medium	Low
Biochemist	X	—	—	—	X	—	X	—	—	X	—	—
Economist	—	—	—	—	—	—	—	—	—	—	—	—
Bank president	—	—	—	—	—	—	—	—	—	—	—	—
Dental hygienist	—	—	—	—	—	—	—	—	—	—	—	—
Military officer	—	—	—	—	—	—	—	—	—	—	—	—
Auto mechanic	—	—	—	—	—	—	—	—	—	—	—	—
Small business owner	—	—	—	—	—	—	—	—	—	—	—	—
Receptionist	—	—	—	—	—	—	—	—	—	—	—	—
Flight attendant	—	—	—	—	—	—	—	—	—	—	—	—
Occupational therapist	—	—	—	—	—	—	—	—	—	—	—	—
Travel agent	—	—	—	—	—	—	—	—	—	—	—	—
Printer	—	—	—	—	—	—	—	—	—	—	—	—
Executive secretary	—	—	—	—	—	—	—	—	—	—	—	—
Chemistry teacher	—	—	—	—	—	—	—	—	—	—	—	—
Magazine editor	—	—	—	—	—	—	—	—	—	—	—	—
Stockbroker	—	—	—	—	—	—	—	—	—	—	—	—
Fashion designer	—	—	—	—	—	—	—	—	—	—	—	—
Construction worker	—	—	—	—	—	—	—	—	—	—	—	—
Cattle farmer	—	—	—	—	—	—	—	—	—	—	—	—
Artist	—	—	—	—	—	—	—	—	—	—	—	—
Judge	—	—	—	—	—	—	—	—	—	—	—	—
Diplomat	—	—	—	—	—	—	—	—	—	—	—	—

Making Connections— Networking

What is a network? Consult any dictionary and after the word "network" you will find definitions describing a number of things, from fabric to communications systems. The common thread through all these definitions is the idea of a sense of support through connections.

Women have been forming social and professional networks for a long time now. Often, women in the same career have helped one another by forming friendships and by making important professional contacts. Right now, you have a potential network of people and organizations that can help you set and achieve your goals—school counselors, teachers, parents, friends of parents, and so on.

MAPPING A NETWORK

Networks evolve naturally as you seek out others with similar interests, concerns, and goals. These informal relationships provide opportunities for mutual support and growth. To illustrate the process, try the following exercise.

Begin by identifying an interest. Now think of at least three people you know who share this interest and list their names on a sheet of paper. Make a second list of others who may not share the interest, but can serve as contacts with people who do. If you are having difficulty naming people, don't forget to check your personal telephone book; after all, it's your portable network record-keeping device.

With these lists of names, you now are ready to map your network. On a blank piece of paper, place your name in the center. Next, write the names of people whom you can contact directly in circles surrounding yours. Then write down those resources that can help you find out about your interest and put triangles around them. Connect your circle to these people and resources with solid lines. Then use boxes to contain the names of people you know who don't share your interest, but who can serve as links to others who do. Connect your circle to these resources with broken lines. The illustration below can be used as your guide. It belongs to Janet MacKenzie, a Senior Girl Scout interested in computers. She mapped a network of people who could help her learn more about computers as a possible career direction.

Shared Interest: Computers

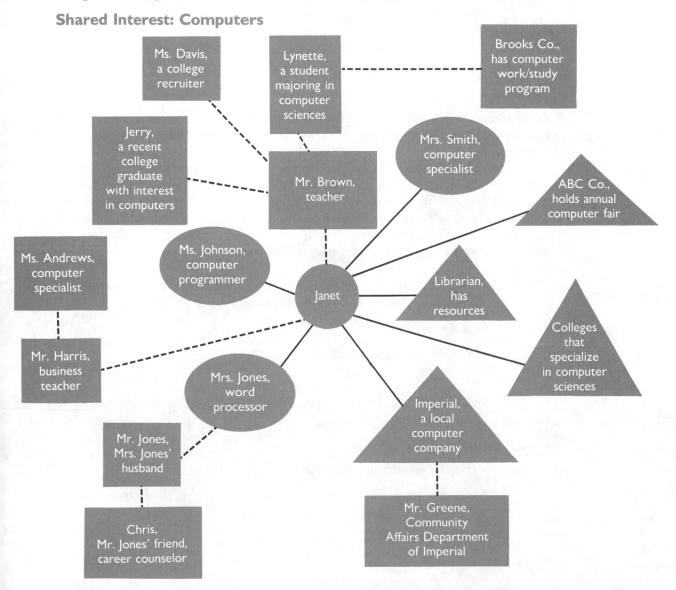

Developing Job-Seeking Skills

WANT ADS

Read the want ads section of your local paper. Which kinds of jobs are available? Select three or four ads and compare them. What are the desired qualifications in terms of experience, education, and skills? How do the jobs compare in salary? Do any of the listed jobs appeal to you?

Many desirable positions are not listed in the want ads. You have to use your networking skills to find out about those jobs. But there is much you can learn from the want ads. A general survey can tell you what types of jobs are in demand and what they pay. You may also get an idea of what personal traits employers are looking for.

Many jobs, no matter how routine they appear, require special talents. Imagine for a moment that you are the personnel officer responsible for hiring staff to fill the following vacancies:

actress	insurance salesperson
office manager	school guidance counselor
air traffic controller	recreational director
camp director	lifeguard
systems analyst	geologist
newspaper reporter	veterinarian

In each case, what sort of person would be an ideal candidate for the job? What personal characteristics should you look for? Share your ideas with other members of your group.

Pick a career that interests you and create your own help wanted ad for the local newspaper. Use your imagination and other resources. Limit yourself to 40 words. And remember, design your ad to attract only those people who have the qualifications and personal attributes that the job requires. What other information will you include in your ad?

Here are some abbreviations that are used in want ads:

aff actn—affirmative action employer, one who seeks and encourages qualified women and minorities to apply for jobs

bkgd—background

col grad—college graduate

deg—degree

eeo—equal employment opportunity, a nondiscriminatory policy of employment

exec—executive

exp nec—experience necessary

f/pd—fee paid; employment agency fee will be paid by employer rather than employee

m/f—male/female

mgmt—management

opty—opportunity

p/t—part time

sal—salary

sal open—salary has not been determined and employer will be flexible

trnee—trainee

wpm—words per minute; refers to typing or stenography speed

w/wo—with/without

20M or 20K—$20,000 salary per year

You might also try creating your own situation wanted ad in which you advertise your skills hoping to attract an employer. Make sure to spell out clearly your best selling points. You might want to mention your personal characteristics, interests, talents, experiences, salary requirements.

Share your ad with a friend. On the basis of the information you provide, she can try to identify at least three careers particularly suited to you. Look through the employment section of your local newspaper. How many help wanted ads match your situation wanted ad?

APPLICATION FORMS

Before going on a job interview, it is a good idea to list all the information you think you may have to provide. The items that you'll probably have to supply include names of schools you've attended with accompanying dates; names, addresses, and dates of former employers; addresses, phone numbers, and titles of people you're using for references (you should always have their permission in advance).

In filling out an application form, always print using blue or black ink. Follow directions carefully—for example, "last name first," "do not write below this line." Do neat work; check for misspellings.

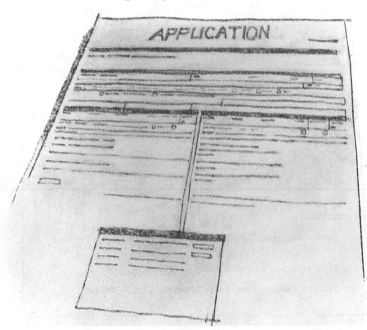

With a friend, collect job application forms from several businesses: a department store, a utility company, a bank, and so on. Practice filling them out and evaluate each other's work.

Visit personnel offices of local companies, especially those that encourage women to enter nontraditional jobs. Or invite personnel officers to visit your troop or group and report what they look for when interviewing applicants. If time allows, troop members can fill out the company's application form, and the personnel office can evaluate some of the completed forms.

WRITING A RÉSUMÉ

A résumé, the written statement you give to a potential employer when you apply for a job, is an essential part of your career life. In a résumé, you present the facts about yourself in a way that shows that you will be able to do the job you are applying for effectively. A résumé tells about your background, experiences, and achievements. Hopefully, it will make you look like the best candidate for the job. Even after the interview, the résumé reminds the employer of your qualifications for the job.

There are several different ways to write a résumé. Below is one type.

RESUME

Veronica Lewis
16 Main Street
Newtown, Ohio 43713
(000) 111-2222

COMMUNICATIONS EXPERIENCE

Researched, wrote, and edited articles for Newtown High
School newspaper as women's sports editor. Contributed
articles to Newtown News school column. President of high
school columnist's club (1985-1986). Directed school play,
Camelot.

COMMUNITY SERVICE

Planned and conducted six one-week summer day-care sessions
for children ages 3 to 5 (1986). Did volunteer work at
Newtown Nursing Home writing letters and reading to residents
(1986-1987). Managed food booth at holiday fair (1986).
Coached Newtown Little League (1986-1987).

SPECIAL ACTIVITIES/AWARDS

Bike-A-Thon for March of Dimes (1983-1987).

Girl Scout Gold Award (1987).

EDUCATION

Newtown High School, Newtown, Ohio. General diploma, 1987.

REFERENCES

Dr. Sandra Robertson, Chairman, English Department, Newtown
High School.

Ms. Ruth Pringle, Managing Editor, Newtown News.

Mr. Richard Lawner, Head Coach, Newtown Little League.

Now, try to write your own résumé highlighting your special skills and stating them in a way that fits the requirements of the career you're interested in. Start by making a complete list of the things you have done. Then pick the ones you think you should emphasize in your résumé.

Here are some hints to use in making your list. Have you ever done any volunteer work? Had a job? Worked with people on a project? Joined a club? Managed anything? Won any awards? Written anything that was published? Sold anything? Performed? Designed and made anything? Won a competition? Fixed anything?

In writing your résumé, use action verbs to describe what you have done. Veronica Lewis used the words "researched," "wrote," "edited," "planned," and "conducted" on her résumé. Here are some other words you might use. This is only a partial list. You can use any other action words you wish.

attended	developed	sold	prepared
made	managed	volunteered	revised
directed	supervised	designed	created

Don't forget to include the things you have done as a Girl Scout on your résumé. Here's your chance to translate all of your accomplishments into information that will get you the job you want.

THE INTERVIEW

The job interview is an important first step toward being hired. It allows the interviewer to see you and to learn first-hand of your strengths and weaknesses as a potential employee in the company. The more prepared and confident you are, the better this process will go for you. Neat attire and punctuality are musts.

In a small group, role-play interviews for specific jobs and evaluate one another. The following questions are frequently asked during job interviews:

- Why did you decide to apply for a position with this company?
- What do you know about our company?
- What qualifications do you have that make you feel you will be successful?
- How would you describe yourself?
- What school courses did you like best? Least? Why?
- Why do you think you would like this particular type of job?
- What do you consider to be your greatest strengths and weaknesses?
- What are your hobbies?
- What are your long-term and short-term goals?
- Why should I hire you?

The following questions can help you to judge your interview performance:

- Did I arrive on time?
- Did I sit up straight and maintain eye contact with the interviewer?
- Was I articulate? Did I speak in complete sentences?
- Was I well-groomed and appropriately dressed?
- Did I leave understanding the nature of the job, the hours, and the salary to be paid?
- Did I refrain from smoking or chewing gum?
- Was I pleasant and courteous?
- Was I able to answer each of the interviewer's questions?
- Did I provide the interviewer with enough information about my experience and strengths?

Following each interview, take the time to write a short thank-you note to your interviewer. You might use this opportunity to mention anything important about yourself that you left out during the actual interview. Also mention that you are looking forward to hearing from her or him.

A Final Word

Women in American society are taking more responsibility for themselves emotionally, intellectually, and economically. You can get off to a good career start by developing all of your interests and abilities while you're young. Become more intellectually aware by reading extensively. Learn more about science and technology so that you become comfortable with these subjects. Try not to specialize too narrowly in your high school or college courses. The world of tomorrow is going to be a better place, and women will play a significant part in making it better!

7

CITIZEN OF THE WORLD

On my honor, I will try:
To serve God and my country,
To help people at all times,
and to live by the Girl Scout Law.

Accepting these words and the ideals which they represent says you care, that you have concerns and are willing to be involved. It also says that you know that your commitment extends far beyond your immediate surroundings. You are a citizen of your community, your state, your country, and your world.

Citizenship is more than just being a resident. Becoming an active citizen requires hard work and a commitment to a better world for all people. This chapter is about the challenge of citizenship and the ways that you can put your talents and skills to work to help others.

Service

Whether you participate in Girl Scouting through a troop, group, or special event, or work independently, service is an integral part of your Girl Scout experience. Service means doing something helpful without the expectation of payment or reward. It is your opportunity to show leadership, to make a difference in the lives of others, and to make a positive impact on your community and your world. In other words, service is a way of relating your experience and knowledge to the needs of others. It is not merely doing something for someone, but helping *when* and *where* you are needed.

There are many ways of volunteering your services to a cause that you believe in, such as working on a teen crisis hotline or working in a senior citizens or child care center. Whatever type of service you choose, the key is involvement. When you read the newspaper or watch the evening news, do you ever wonder how you might fit in? What is your responsibility to the people of your community? What can you do to help?

If you take some time and look around you'll see things that need doing: in your neighborhood, in your school, in the environment. Do you want to wait for things to happen? Or do you want to turn your concern for the social ills and issues facing your community into action? Make things happen, things that make a difference.

Issues for Girl Scouts

With each coming year your knowledge and understanding about yourself and your world will continue to grow. So too will your commitment to issues that concern you and your ability to be an active volunteer. There are many issues you may not be able to deal with until sometime in the future. But right now, you have the opportunity to put your skills and talents into action to improve the quality of life for yourself and for others with whom you share this planet. The following sections can help you decide where you might direct your talents and energy.

Environmental Concerns

Girl Scouting has always recognized the need to protect the earth and the life it supports. As today's Girl Scout and tomorrow's community leader, you can help protect, preserve, and improve the environment.

The earth's physical environment and all its living creatures are an interconnected whole. Any change, whether small or large, has an impact. Sometimes environmental changes are large and sudden and beyond anyone's control, such as when a volcano erupts or there is an earthquake. Or, an environmental change may be largely due to human ignorance or carelessness, such as a forest fire caused by a discarded burning cigarette.

At other times, changes and disturbances to the environment may build over time. Acid rain has become a global problem as the factories of industrialized areas dump pollutant smoke into the atmosphere. Even on a small scale, there is a need to protect what we have or take action when a problem occurs. The gradual erosion of community park land can leave little for future children to enjoy. The effect of a local oil spill can be greatly reduced if concerned citizens move in quickly to help.

Taking a protective stand for the environment doesn't just mean responding to a crisis. There are many ways to prevent environmental problems. Using our natural resources wisely, being alert to potential problems, knowing about the needs of plant and animal life are all ways to protect and improve our surroundings.

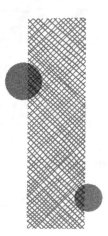

ACTIVITIES

■ Conduct a water-saver campaign in your home. Develop a list of ways to stop water pollution and work with appropriate agencies to enforce clean-up.

■ Select a natural resource that has particular significance to your community. Determine the different ways it has an impact on the community. Survey the community to find out who is most dependent on the resource.

■ Join with other Girl Scout troops or service organizations to do an extended conservation project. Consider the following natural resources: water, air, fuels and energy sources, minerals and metals, soil, food crops, wood.

■ Do some of the activities in the Contemporary Issues booklet, *Earth Matters*. See the *Earth Matters* slide show to get more ideas about what can be done.

Investigate the major uses of each resource and whether they have synthetic substitutes.

LOU HENRY HOOVER MEMORIAL SANCTUARIES

Lou Henry Hoover Memorial Sanctuary projects were established in 1944 by the GSUSA National Board of Directors as a living memorial to Lou Henry Hoover, wife of Herbert Hoover, the former President of the United States. She was an active Girl Scout from her investiture by Juliette Low in 1917 to her death in 1943. She served twice as elected President of GSUSA and once as Honorary President.

During her years in Girl Scouting, Lou Henry Hoover worked enthusiastically to enlarge the scope of Girl Scout program in the out-of-doors. This interest is built into the design of Lou Henry Hoover Memorial Sanctuaries.

A Lou Henry Hoover Memorial Sanctuary is any natural area designated by a council for the purpose of providing a setting where Girl Scouts can gain an understanding of the interrelationships of all forms of life. Girls must play a part in analyzing, planning, developing, and managing the site. The initial plan for development and management must cover a five-year period.

ELLIOTT WILDLIFE VALUES PROJECT

The Elliott Wildlife Values Project, launched by Girl Scouts of the U.S.A. in 1977, represents the hopes and dreams of one individual for preserving wildlife in the United States. The late Herford N. Elliott of Massachusetts felt strongly about making young people aware of the senseless killing of animals for sport and amusement. He provided a trust fund to Girl Scouts of the U.S.A. to design and implement wildlife education projects.

Wildlife education develops awareness, knowledge, skills, and commitment; the result is informed decisions, responsible behavior, and constructive actions toward wildlife. Councils have been encouraged to use their outdoor sites as learning laboratories and to enhance wildlife habitats. Many councils also operate camps, nature centers, and events where you can learn more about protecting wildlife.

Encourage your troop or group to look for service opportunities with local conservation and environmental organizations. Plan a community service project that will help people appreciate the wildlife in your area. *Outdoor Education in Girl Scouting* and *Exploring Wildlife Communities with Children* are two resources that provide many activities you could use while working with a younger troop or while enjoying outdoor activities yourself. Follow up your interest in conservation by doing an interest project in this area.

Human Relations

People need people. They need to care about each other, work to understand and respect each other, and they need to make extra efforts for each other when difficulties or crises arise. Throughout your life, you may encounter or hear about situations of adversity or misfortune. There is always the opportunity for you to make a difference. Right now there are millions of people living in difficult situations and many who face life-threatening problems. You can contribute to the health and well-being of countless individuals as well as your own.

Prejudice

To be prejudiced against a person or group of people is to make judgments about them before getting to know them. These prejudged attitudes can be based on many different things: dress, social status, age, sex, religion, skin color, disabilities.

Prejudging a person on the way she dresses, for example, is making a decision about her character, abilities, and talents based on outward appearance. In reality, a person's outside appearance does not indicate how she feels and thinks on the inside.

Why are some people prejudiced and other people more accepting of others? Often, prejudice evolves out of fear. People tend to fear what they don't know. They avoid the hard work of becoming acquainted with those who have different backgrounds. Prejudice may be learned in our society from the media, from interaction with others, even from our parents and neighbors. To be more open to others, you must accept people even though they differ from you. We all have a lot to learn from each other, and when we do strip away the external differences such as dress and skin color, we can discover some common basis for friendship.

What You Can Do

■ Know that everybody has a rich, complex culture to be proud of. To consider any ethnic group "culturally deprived" is inaccurate.
■ Know that you can accept others as equal human beings without agreeing with them about everything.
■ Do not prejudge those who are different from you. Become a positive model for others to follow. This is especially good for younger children, who often try to imitate your behavior.
■ Complete some of the activities in the Contemporary Issues booklet, *Valuing Differences: Promoting Pluralism.*

PREJUDICE AND LANGUAGE

Many prejudicial attitudes are ingrained in our language. Common sayings and expressions may have meanings and associations that reflect a prejudicial attitude. Think about instances where language reflects notions about a racial, religious, or ethnic group. Discuss each term and decide whether it has a positive or negative meaning. Make a pact with yourself and others not to use terms that carry prejudices.

MYTHS AND FAIRY TALES

Prejudicial attitudes are also found in art and literature. Find three examples of prejudice in art and literature. For example, reread several European fairy tales and folk tales that have characters with disabilities. Make a list of the stories and the characters.

Describe how the characters with disabilities are depicted: heroic, intelligent, good, cowardly, stupid, evil, or weak. How are stepparents and poor people depicted? What have you discovered?

Do this with a partner or a group. Compare your findings. Did people with different backgrounds find different examples?

STEREOTYPING

A stereotype is a general belief, usually negative, about all members of a particular group of people. The general belief grows out of misunderstanding and ignorance. As with prejudice, stereotyping involves prejudging. If it applies to some *individuals* of a group, the stereotype is labeled true for *all members* of that group. Examples of stereotypes are: Fat people are happy and jolly . . . Deaf people are dumb . . . Old people are cranky . . . Women are bad drivers . . . Teenagers are irresponsible.

Stereotypical beliefs interfere with our true appreciation of diverse people. Find examples of stereotyping, and with a group discuss what is wrong with the stereotype and what can be done to prevent it in the future.

Stereotyping and Dislikes

Do you have to like everybody and everything? It is unrealistic to expect you to. What you should expect of each other and of yourself, is that you face each person with an open mind and an accepting spirit. Only then will you allow yourself to become acquainted with the real person and to form a more accurate opinion of that person as an individual.

Many times stereotypes grow out of experiences that have been intense or repeated. For example, a big homework assignment three weekends in a row might translate into "Teachers don't like kids to have fun." Or several arguments with your retired neighbor become "Old people are mean and cranky."

Think about stereotyped views that you hold. How did they develop? Work to change those views.

Examine current magazines, advertisements, television programs, children's books, etc., for evidence of stereotyping and negative portrayals of racial and ethnic groups or women. Ask yourself these questions:

1. Does the material contain negative messages or images about a particular group?
2. Are the lifestyles or abilities shown as inferior?
3. Are the illustrations of physical features unrealistic, such as yellow skin for Asians? Are people of one racial or ethnic group portrayed in a stereotypical manner (that is, all looking alike)?
4. Are they portrayed as passive? defenseless? dependent? unattractive? Do they have decision-making positions?

Discrimination

To discriminate against people is to act toward them on the basis of prejudice. We can find as many different reasons to discriminate as we find to be prejudiced: people are too fat, too tall, too old or young; they wear glasses, have dark skin, pale skin, are male or female; they worship differently, live in different neighborhoods, come from different countries. Our prejudices divide and separate us from each other. Discrimination carries these prejudices one step further. It closes the door of opportunity to those being discriminated against, and stereotypes are often used to justify discrimination.

Historically women have been victims of discrimination. Many have had to fight for the right to vote, to be educated, to gain entrance in certain schools and careers. Women have also had to live down stereotypes. It was commonly believed that females were obedient and passive, that they could not excel in science and math, and that a woman's place was only in the home.

We know that things have gotten better for women, particularly in the work world, but the Bureau of Census shows that a man with a bachelor's degree can still expect to earn twice as much in a lifetime as a woman with a bachelor's degree. Even taking into account the work interruptions that many women have, the earnings gap would be reduced by only 15 percent. Males, white males in particular, earn more money and have more social power than females or people of color.

The stereotypes of older people as mentally slow, sickly, or "old-fashioned" have led to discrimination against them in the work world and, in some cases, to an inability to get good medical care. Employers have discriminated against them because of the mistaken belief that they all lack mental alertness. The aged are often taken advantage of and are victims of crime. The young often exclude the old from their lives, which means that both are deprived of rich experiences.

Another example of discrimination is that based on skin color and race. Like most other forms of discrimination, racial discrimination can be found in housing, schools, businesses, the government, and the media.

However, even a small change in awareness and open-mindedness on your part can contribute toward ending such discrimination. Don't underestimate your influence. What you say and do affects those around you. You can be assertive about your feelings (see pages 69–70). Speak up, respond, react when negative feelings and emotions are expressed around you.

ACTIVITIES

Survey television programs, children's books, work situations, and U.S. history for examples of discrimination with regard to sex, race, age, and religion. You can work in groups, dividing up the categories. Spend a troop or group meeting time reporting and discussing your results.

Role-play the following situations:

■ A woman who is a single parent speaks to her boss, asserting her right to make as much money as the male workers do.
■ A teenaged girl and her boyfriend disagree about her taking an auto mechanics class.
■ An American Indian teenager overhears two White girls laughing about a racist joke. She speaks to them about it (a White person should take the role of the American Indian).
■ A senior citizen is interviewed for a job as a department store salesperson. The interviewer is reluctant about hiring an older person.

Make up some situations of your own to role-play.

People with Disabilities

People with disabilities in increasing numbers are taking their place alongside people without disabilities. Society is recognizing that a person's one difference is less important than all her similarities; as with race, sex, and other ways we have of dividing ourselves into "them" and "us," disability barriers are wearing down. But, there are still many situations and circumstances in which people with disabilities face discrimination.

As a result of antidiscrimination bills that went into effect in the 1970s, adults

and children with disabilities are now more visible on accessible transportation systems, in schools, and in other public places and worksites. You may have a disability or know someone who does. If so, you should know that disabilities do not mean that career goals as well as personal development goals cannot be achieved. In almost every occupation there are people with disabilities. They are your role models.

As a friend, how can you show respect to a person with a disability? Here is what your peers with disabilities have to say:

Sidney, who is deaf: "Some of my friends had trouble understanding me at first, and a couple of people were even scared of me. My speech is not clear because I've never heard words pronounced. But, after being around me for a while, people feel more comfortable. Now I'm just one of the guys."

Ruth, who is blind: "Until last year, I attended a school for the blind where people were just like me. Now I am mainstreamed in a regular school. One of the worst things about being blind is people's reactions. They sometimes leave us out of things because they feel we don't understand. Well, I like to be treated the same as anybody else as much as that is possible. I like people and I'm happy that the kids at my school like and accept me."

Addie, who lost her right leg: "I lost my leg in a car accident. From the knee down, I wear a prosthesis, which is an artificial body part. As I get taller, I get new longer ones. Some people choose not to wear a prosthesis, but I'm glad I have mine. I can run and ride a bike. Whenever I feel sorry for myself, my father reminds me that I'm still the same on the inside and that's what really counts."

People with disabilities have a physical or mental impairment that makes doing certain things more difficult. Some disabilities may be mild, others severe; some may be visible, others difficult to detect. The important thing to understand is that a disability need not be a barrier. A disability means that certain things are harder to do or have to be done differently. Everyone has a variety of talents and abilities. A disability in one area does not mean all the others are affected. Between people with disabilities and people without, mutual understanding and respect are essential. Here are some ideas to help bring about that understanding and respect:

■ Become an active partner in mainstreaming—that is, support people with disabilities as they take their part in regular activities in your community, at school, and in Girl Scouting. If you have a disability, you can promote understanding; if you don't have a disability, you can lend needed support.
■ Educate others. Ignorance and insensitivity are two of the greatest barriers faced by people with disabilities.
■ Highlight the lives of people of accomplishment who have had a disability: Franklin Roosevelt, Juliette Low, Ludwig van Beethoven, Helen Keller are some you might know about.
■ Design ways to provide support that would help persons with disabilities.
■ Survey facilities that have barriers for people with disabilities. Help construct barrier-free environments.

- Start a disability support group. Invite youths with disabilities to participate in some of your troop/group activities. Extend friendship to those who are new to your neighborhood or school.
- Ask someone with a disability (either a child or an adult) to teach you a skill or hobby that she or he is good at.
- Invite an occupational therapist to talk to your group about her job of preparing people with disabilities to reenter occupations.
- Look through the book *Focus on Ability* to learn more about the different types of disabilities that people may have. Share what you learn with others.

Intergenerational Exchange

An intergenerational exchange is any activity or program that involves sharing knowledge, skills, or experience between generations. Children, parents, and grandparents represent three different generations. Intergenerational sharing provides the link between older persons who possess a lifetime of knowledge and skills, and younger persons who possess energy and new knowledge. Many communities have developed intergenerational programs in schools, churches and synagogues, businesses and clubs. The success of these programs has resulted in an improvement in the academic and social abilities of youth, as well as in increased mental and physical health and self-esteem for senior citizens.

The Intergenerational Education Volunteer Network Act was introduced in Congress in 1985. It provides for programs that enable senior citizens to work with educationally disadvantaged children.

The purposes are to upgrade the basic skills of these children by placing volunteers in the schools and homes, and to create a link between schools and communities, thus enriching the lives of both younger and older Americans.

You can start an intergenerational program. Begin by taking an informal survey of some of the senior citizens in your community. What skills do they have? What are their interests? You will see for yourself how varied senior citizens are when it comes to personality, abilities, talents, and interests. Then decide on activity ideas that will offer young people a chance to work with older people, to learn from them and with them. You can provide services to older people, and older people can provide services to younger people; both groups can work together cooperatively.

Some ideas to consider are:

1. Program consultants. Senior citizens share their cultural and educational resources with a group of Girl Scouts.
2. Apprenticeships. Senior citizens work with small groups of youths on a craft or hobby for a specific period of time. This arrangement can be repeated with different groups of youths.
3. Pen pals. Girls write to nursing home residents, visiting them and inviting them to attend school or troop functions such as plays, fairs, and concerts.
4. Grandparenting a self-care child (a youngster who is home alone after school). Self-care children are matched up with a neighborhood "grandparent." The children can call the volunteer when they arrive home or when they have a problem. They can establish a lasting relationship, especially if they live nearby.
5. Teen escorts. Girls accompany senior citizens to the bank, to stores, and to doctor appointments.

Pluralism

You live in a pluralistic society—a society in which numerous distinct ethnic, religious, and cultural groups coexist to form one nation of people, our United States of America. The strength of our nation and its success in the world have come from the contributions of these different groups. You can gain a pluralistic attitude through an appreciation of the diversity in people.

Gaining respect for diverse people and lifestyles is as important internationally as it is nationally. The world has become interdependent. For a period in American history, we adopted a policy of isolation and cut ourselves off from the rest of the world. No country on earth can afford to live that way now. The world affects you and you affect the world. You share a common future with people all over the earth as local and national issues such as environment, education, and peace have become international issues.

Literacy

Millions of people in the United States and throughout the world are unable to read or read at a very low level. Girl Scouts in the United States can do their part to promote literacy, whether it be a simple program of self-improvement, involvement on a community level, or linkage with an international effort.

ACTIVITIES

■ Develop a personal or family reading improvement campaign.
■ Plan activities to support reading among your friends—sharing of personal journals, a reading hour once a month, volunteer tutoring with other Girl Scouts.
■ Get involved in a library or school program that supports reading and the development of reading skills.
■ Identify priority literacy needs in your council. For example, there may be a number of non-English-speaking people who want to learn to read in English.
■ Enlist the aid of educators, public library personnel, and volunteers to design a curriculum or reading list and to promote literacy activities. Arrange for activities in a variety of locations and at different times to allow easy access for the target population. Libraries, community centers, and churches can be used to house an ongoing literacy program.
■ With the help of early childhood educators, develop a reading

readiness program for young children. Join with existing community groups to provide tutoring for older children and adults.

- Provide English-language (written and oral) tutoring for persons preparing to become citizens. Focus on learning to use telephone books and street maps and on other life skills that require reading.
- Do some of the activities in the *Right to Read* Contemporary Issues booklet.

Health Concerns

The entire issue of health presents a great variety of opportunities to give service. You might find that prevention or health maintenance programs would be the perfect outlet for your energies. Or you might like to put your skills to work aiding those who are critically ill. Whatever the cause, you can make a difference. Start today to think how you can help. Look at the health needs in your community. What are your talents and how can they be matched to an area where help is needed? Start thinking about potential service projects related to health care. Here are some ideas:

- Promote physical fitness. Being physically fit is one way to maintain health. Start an exercise program for younger children. Build a fitness trail in a community recreation area.
- Prevent substance abuse. Drug and alcohol abuse are a major threat to our nation's health. Teach others. Promote public awareness of the problem. Support efforts to prevent drunk driving. Ask your leader about GSUSA's *Tune In to Well-Being, Say No to Drugs*.
- Do research to learn what service organizations—such as the World Health Organization, UNICEF, CARE, Save the Children, and religious missions—are doing to improve health care in this country.
- Help your troop or group to identify a health care problem that affects your community. Develop a plan that enables the girls to become part of the solution.
- Work with the library or civic associations to identify a health care concern in a developing nation. Find out how health care is provided and whether these services meet the needs of the people.

"To Help Where I Am Needed"

Many instances of people needing help don't fall into a specific category. Needs vary from community to community and from year to year. If you know your talents and values, you will always find a way to help.

Be sensitive to the world around you and the issues that concern you. You can help with:

homelessness	illiteracy	crime and violence	animal welfare
urban blight	prejudice	substance abuse	loneliness
hunger	children in crisis	unemployment	pollution

Focus your ideas. What changes would you like to see as a result of the efforts of yourself and others? Pick out something you'd like to do. You have to start somewhere.

TAKE ACTION

Service projects can take many forms. They can be worked on individually or in groups. You might be able to bring about some real changes yourself or you can be an agent of change—working to influence those in positions of power. Some service projects are short-term, while others may take many months.

Whatever the issue that concerns you, you can make a difference. In some cases you may work locally and see immediate results. At other times progress may be small and steady. It is important to never lose sight of your goals and to know that no matter how big or small your cause, your efforts will help. Here are some simple steps to take.

1. Help educate others.
2. Become an issues expert. Learn a great deal about an issue that concerns you.
3. Determine ways you can pitch in and help.
4. Network with others: individuals, groups, organizations.
5. Join forces with others who can help you achieve your goals.
6. Learn how to express your concerns with legislators and government officials who can help shape future directions.
7. Keep working on your goals.

PLANNING A SERVICE PROJECT

Look around and see where you can make a difference using your special skills, interest, and commitment. If you want to start something new in your school, town, or neighborhood, or perhaps stop something, how will you let people know about your idea? Who will help you get the action started? What are some of the problems you might face? What are some of the topics that could become the focus of your project?

Step #1

Focus your ideas: What changes would you like to see? Decide on one thing you'd really like to do.

Step #2

Begin your planning by filling in the following blanks:

One thing that really needs doing: _____

_____

_____

One or more realistic goals for my service project is/are: _____

_____

_____

Skills and interests I can apply to this project are: _____

_____

_____

People I can work with on this project are: _____

_____

_____

Steps I can take to get this project started:

1. _____

_____

2. _____

_____

3. _____

_____

To do what you want to do, you will most likely have to overcome obstacles, change direction, try several approaches. Consider how you might handle the situation if someone says:

> "Your ideas won't work."
> "I'm too busy to see you now."
> "No one cares about that problem."
> "We don't want your help."

Step #3

Along with a lot of determination and persistence, you will need some help with your project. List people who can help you develop your ideas. Recruit others who can help clear red tape or work with you directly. Keep their names, addresses, and telephone numbers in a convenient location.

People who can help with this project:

Name	Address	Telephone Number	Type of Help

As you develop your plan, make sure:

- You are meeting a need in the community.
- Your goals are realistic and attainable.
- You have kept to the principles of the Girl Scout Promise and Law.
- Your plan of action is spelled out so that everyone involved knows who does what and when.

Step #4

If your project involves working with another agency or organization, determine the specific details in advance: beginning date, whether training will be given, materials needed, transportation arrangements, dress codes, hours, and length of service.

Financing Your Plans

Generally, a service project can be carried out within a troop's or group's budget. But what about those big ideas you have? Those tremendous plans for ways to make your community a safer, healthier, happier, and more beautiful place? What will happen to those ideas if your troop's/group's budget is down to zero? If your project calls for financial resources that you don't have, you might want to plan a money-earning project.

Troop money-earning activities are opportunities for your troop to get money by making and selling a product or offering your skills in a particular area for a fee. These activities/projects are planned and carried out through the efforts of girls in partnership with adults. The activities take into consideration each girl's abilities, interests, and willingness to participate. For any troop money-earning project, the troop must first have the written permission of the council. Other regulations and guidelines that must be checked before starting your project are described in *Safety-Wise*, which is available to your Girl Scout leader or adviser.

The following are examples of ideas for activities that could help your troop raise money.

Collecting newspapers or
bottles and cans for recycling

Washing cars

Puppet shows

Household work

Art shows

Craft sales

Garage sales

Flea markets

In some cases, you may want to seek co-sponsors of your project among other groups in the community. Co-sponsors are businesses, service groups, civic organizations, or religious groups that are willing to support your project by donating their time, money, equipment, or professional expertise.

Your first step is to contact your council through your adult partner to get approval of your plans. Then, set up appointments to tell potential co-sponsors about your project and solicit their support in helping you reach your goals. Ask for their suggestions, as well as their help. Who knows what the outcome might be? For example, there may be added opportunities and advantages that aren't apparent at first.

Be original in your approach! For example, plans with the Parks Department for a physical fitness trail in a city park might just get help from the early morning joggers who stop to read eye-catching posters along their way. Your Girl Scout council office, your library, or your local chamber of commerce may be able to provide information about community groups whose interests and concerns are similar to yours.

READER'S DIGEST GRANTS FOR COMMUNITY SERVICE

For over twenty years, Girl Scouts have been making the world a better place to live with the help of Reader's Digest. Each year since 1964, Reader's Digest has provided funds to support community service projects developed by girls. This money has enabled many Cadette and Senior Girl Scout troops to carry out projects that they might not otherwise have had the finances to complete.

Projects over the years have included clean-ups of local parks, playgrounds, and lakes; after-school tutorial programs; camp experiences for children with disabilities; fire safety workshops for children; and many others.

To apply for a grant, contact your local Girl Scout council office to obtain application forms and guidelines on how and when to apply. In the application, describe in your own words, the people, skills, time, and money the project will require. You describe the need for the project and how your plans will meet that need, setting a beginning date for the project. If you are funded, you must submit a complete report of the activity and a financial report at the end of the grant period.

Service Training

In Girl Scouting, you have an opportunity to attend special training sessions that prepare you to give service in a certain area. The skills that are developed in training can be very useful later in life, especially as you embark on a career. Your leader or your council office can provide you with information about various types of service training that are available through your council.

Girl Scouts give service without expectation of payment or reward. When you participate in a service training, you are entitled to receive a Service Training bar that you may wear when you give service. This bar signifies that you have learned how to work in a specific area. Once you have completed the training, you fulfill a commitment to give at least 25 hours of service in the area in which you have been trained. More information about Service Training bars is on page 152.

Service Training bars

Active Citizenship

In a democratic society, individuals exercise their right to direct and determine what life will be like in the future. Young Americans can help shape the world they will enter as adults.

VOTING RIGHTS

Young Americans can lobby for reforms in their own interest or in the interest of the next generation. What has happened in the past, what is happening now, will have an impact on the future. For example: If today's generation fails to safely dispose of toxic wastes, tomorrow's adults will suffer. If we do not seek ways to replenish current natural resources, the standard of living enjoyed today will be at an incredible expense to the next generation.

You may not be old enough to vote yourself, but you are old enough to begin to be involved in the democratic process. If you don't vote, help someone who can, perhaps by organizing a group of baby-sitters or a transportation pool to enable registered voters to exercise their right. Find out about voter registration—get involved.

You can become involved at many levels by being active in and knowledgeable about what is going on in your local community and your state as well as on the national and even the international scene.

- Brainstorm important issues that your generation will have to face.
- Discuss and debate current events, including the issues you identified while brainstorming.
- Learn about the law and citizens' rights.
- Know who your elected representatives are. Find out about how government works in your community.
- Discuss ways in which you can help shape future directions—helping others vote, making educational posters and displays, holding discussion forums to help others become involved.
- Learn about and educate others on issues that affect you. Your input can influence the fate of important legislation that will affect the quality of your life and the lives of others.
- Learn about the naturalization process. Find out what people are required to know in order to become United States citizens. Attend a naturalization ceremony if possible, or role-play both the naturalization exam and the ceremony.

Think Globally, Act Locally

You may find that your interests and concerns for developing a service project extend beyond working on a neighborhood traffic light. Many young women your age find that they are concerned with issues and problems that have a broader scope than their immediate communities. After all, the phrase "to help people at all times" challenges us to address the many current global concerns that face us all today. We all hear and know something about these issues—homelessness, illiteracy, hunger, environmental pollution, deforestation.

Although these problems are global, we can begin solving them by taking action locally.

By thinking globally and acting locally, you can make a measurable difference in the quality of life for yourself and others. There are ways to work in your own community and make an impact on global and national concerns.

MULTICULTURAL AWARENESS

Our global interdependence forces people together. As an American and as a Girl Scout, you will need to interact and cooperate with people from different cultures within this country and outside of it. You will learn that people from different backgrounds observe and evaluate the world differently. As you interact with others, you will learn how to deal with differences. You will be able to identify what is valuable in the cultures of others.

What is meant by "culture"? Culture refers to the acceptable behavior, values, and beliefs of a group of people as expressed in the group's customs, traditions, religions, literature, art, clothing, and so forth. Culture is everything that makes up the life of a people. Although it may be related to a racial or ethnic group, culture also may be present in any collection of people who operate as a group. By this definition, your Girl Scout group is a culture with values and standards of behavior that are passed on to new members.

The best way to learn a culture's traditions is to see them through someone who knows and practices them. It is more difficult to learn a culture's values. Values are displayed indirectly by the way people act in different situations— their behavior, gestures, and tone of voice. And of course there is much individual variation within a cultural group: every member of a cultural group does not have identical values and preferences.

GLOBAL PERSPECTIVES

There are many technologically underdeveloped countries in Africa, Asia, and Latin America. The economies of these countries often are based upon an agricultural system. These countries, frequently referred to as third world countries, have many people who daily face hunger, drought, and diseases.

One of the questions confronting us all is, "How can we enable citizens of all nations to live decent lives?" In many cities, more than a million homeless people live without sanitation, clean piped water, garbage removal, schools, roads, and health centers. The conditions of life faced by many third world people are even more tragic when you consider their rich heritages. Many Latin Americans are descendants of the Aztecs and Incas, who had thriving empires and structured societies rich in technological and artistic achievements. Africa ushered in the Bronze Age thousands of years ago, with complex economic and transportation systems. On both continents today, ruins stand as reminders of their magnificent past.

Third world people continue to have rich and complex cultures. Increase your appreciation and understanding of diverse cultures by traveling, reading, viewing films, and learning more. Many American cities have ethnic festivals, restaurants, markets, and museum exhibits, where you can learn more about the art, food, and customs of many ethnic groups.

Activities

■ Select a cultural group you would like to learn more about. Study it by reading books, magazines, and by talking to members of that group (or if that isn't possible, by contacting people who have studied the cultural group). Consider language, lifestyle practices, religions, customs, medicine, recreation, attitudes, laws, education, literature, art, dance, music, games, food, and dress.

■ Prepare lists of products (clothing, food ingredients, appliances, etc.) from other countries that you use every day. Spend some time in a grocery store or department store. Record the products and their countries of origin.

■ Read your local paper for articles describing decisions or activities abroad that may affect your life. Discuss how they could affect you or the people in your community.

■ Adopt a third world city. Learn as much as you can about the way people live, work, feel. Go beyond their holidays, foods, and ceremonies to learn about their everyday life.

■ Learn about diverse lifestyles in your own country. Consider the lifestyles of miners, ranchers, farmers, Native Americans on reservations, residents of Appalachia, Alaskan Eskimos.

■ Create a world government where each member represents a different cultural group (either an American ethnic group or a foreign cultural group). Issue a world passport for international citizenship. Decide on problems or issues affecting world citizens, and see what possible solutions exist.

Global Issues

As a Girl Scout, you are a part of a worldwide network that shares your commitment to helping people. Even if you were not aware of it at the time, when you became a registered member of Girl Scouts of the U.S.A. you began to think globally and act locally. Your Girl Scout membership means that you are part of an international organization, the World Association of Girl Guides and Girl Scouts (WAGGGS). In fact, you are a part of the largest voluntary organization for girls and women in the world.

As Girl Guides and Girl Scouts, you share with over eight million others the basic principles embodied in the Promise and Law as well as a consciousness that, in many instances, the universal problems that we hear about on the news are very real problems in the daily lives of our sister Girl Guides and Girl Scouts. Service is one of our universal links to WAGGGS. Girl Guides and Girl Scouts put their skills and experiences into action to meet the needs of their community.

If you were to visit a world center, or perhaps go on an international wider opportunity, you would notice many differences and similarities in the way other Girl Guides and Girl Scouts do things. What is important about WAGGGS is the universal effort to address the problems and needs of young women striving to reach their fullest potential.

In particular, the World Association has taken a special interest in promotion of child health. The concept of service to others combined with concern for good health has many implications for Girl Guides and Girl Scouts all over the world.

The four key needs related to the health of women and children in many third world countries are:

■ Growth monitoring charts for mothers to identify malnutrition
■ Oral rehydration therapy to prevent death from diarrhea
■ Education about breast feeding and nutrition
■ Immunization against common diseases

ACTIVITIES

Assess your resources and think about ways in which you can make a difference. Here are some ideas:

■ With the assistance of your Girl Scout council, link up with a community health care project. For information and materials, write to Group Programs, U.S. Committee for UNICEF, 331 East 38th Street, New York, N.Y. 10016.
■ Conduct an event for World Health Day (April 7) with a fair or information booth.

■ Research the issue of worldwide hunger—why it exists, what factors contribute—by contacting such organizations as UNICEF, CARE, and the World Hunger Education Office.

■ Find out about community organizations that are involved in working to end worldwide hunger.

■ Explore careers in the field by interviewing social service workers, UNICEF officials, religious workers, food program employees.

■ Follow hunger-related issues in the news (for example, the infant formula controversy, or the export of grain to other countries).

Working Together Toward Peace

Many people consider peace to be a passive state instead of an active process. Action is most often associated with conflict. But peace can be active too—it may represent joy and excitement, caring for someone, and working with others toward a worthwhile goal. It is the challenge of sports competition, the cleaning of the environment, and the bridging of cultural differences. Peace is many things. Think about what peace means to you.

PEACE JOURNAL

Write about a time or a way that you personally experienced peace. For one week or longer, keep a peace journal. In it, express such feelings as:

1. What are your hopes for peace in your life?
2. Does seeking peace mean being nonviolent?
3. What is the relationship between inner peace and outer peace-making?
4. Remember a time when you felt very close to another person.
5. Remember a time when you felt inspired and joyous.

BE A PEACEMAKER . . .

1. in your family by giving advice and support or by listening.
2. in your community by planning and carrying out a service project (see pages 115–119).
3. in the World of the Arts by listening to music, reading poetry, and viewing art that sends messages of peace to you; or creating your own peace song, poem, montage, or poster to share with others.

CONDUCT A PEACE INTERVIEW

Suggested questions are:

1. What words, images, or situations come to your mind when you think of peace?

2. What is your definition of peace?

3. Are you doing anything to bring about peace in your community, country, or the world?

■ For three days keep track of daily TV or newspaper stories that are based on conflict, violence, and peace. How many are there in each category?

■ Watch several TV shows that have a great deal of conflict and violence. How are these conflicts resolved in the various shows?

■ Do you think violence and conflict are promoted by the media?

Remember that you have an important part in shaping the future of our world. As a peacemaker, you will help shape it in a positive way.

The World of Tomorrow

Thinking globally and acting locally is one way to improve your world. Yours will be the world of the 21st century. How do you envision it? A global village free from disease, poverty, racism, and hunger? Or a world overrun by these universal problems? What are you doing to help make the world an acceptable place for you and your family?

Did you know that:

■ Two out of three of the world's illiterates are women, and one out of five American adults cannot read or write.

■ Girls in the U.S.A. continue to lag behind boys in computer literacy.

■ On the average, American women earn less than men earn, even when they hold similar jobs.

■ More than half of all U.S women are in the paid work force either full- or part-time.

■ The racial and ethnic minority populations in the United States continue to increase in number. By the turn of the century, 30 percent of the American population is expected to be comprised of racial and ethnic minorities, up from 22 percent in the mid-1980s.

What are some of the implications of these statistics? What can you do to make a difference? What issues or concerns could a well-developed service project address?

As we face the turn of the century, we should reflect to see if we are keeping the same high-spirited pace Juliette Low did when she founded Girl Scouting in the United States. She was ready to withstand criticism of her progressive thinking. She did not let the status quo keep her from moving ahead with her forward-thinking ideas and ideals for women. Are your views and ideas on human relations—women, peace, age—as forward-looking as our founder's were? If not, what can you do—individually and collectively—to improve them? You might initiate activities or discussions that help build a positive self-identity racially, culturally, and sexually. Learn about women and other cultures. These issues will impact on your future sooner than you realize. Prepare yourself and your community to enter into the global village with a positive, uplifting attitude toward getting along with others.

8

WIDER OPPORTUNITIES

Wider opportunities are just what the words would lead you to expect. They are opportunities for experiences beyond your circle of family, friends, and Girl Scout troop or group members. Girls learn about themselves and their world by participating in wider opportunity activities, projects, or events with other Girl Scouts who are in a different troop, group, or council than their own. Lord Baden-Powell, founder of the Boy Scouts, believed that you could gain a greater understanding of the world by looking beyond yourself. His quote, "Look wide and when you think you're looking wide, look wider still," inspired the term wider opportunities.

Wider opportunities are for Girl Scouts of all ages. For Daisy Girl Scouts a wider opportunity can be a trip to the zoo, for Brownie Girl Scouts it can be an overnight camping trip, for Junior Girl Scouts it can be a weekend trip. For Cadette and Senior Girl Scouts, the list of choices and possibilities is almost endless.

Archaeology, backpacking, canoeing, computers, horseback riding, medicine, music, and photography are just some examples of interests that you may be able to explore through wider opportunities close to home, in another state, or even abroad.

Wider opportunities can include non-Girl Scouts and community organizations as well as Girl Scouts and Girl Guides from different countries. When you participate in a wider opportunity, you will explore a variety of interests and activities—meet new people and experience exciting things.

There are several ways to be involved in a wider opportunity. Whether you are a participant or part of the planning team, you'll find great rewards. Below are some examples of the range of wider opportunities.

Some wider opportunities close to home might be:

- One troop invites another to participate in a film festival they have planned.
- A troop or group and another troop or group join together to plan a trip to the state capital to explore state government at work.
- Several troops join in a project to make a park trail accessible for people with disabilities.
- Your troop and a Senior Citizen Community Center create a play and put on a performance with senior citizens.
- Girl Scouts in the neighborhood hold an international festival, inviting community members to participate.
- Your council sponsors a councilwide winter sports event for all Girl Scouts.
- Two neighboring councils bring together Girl Scouts throughout the area to attend a statewide leadership conference.

Some wider opportunities away from home might be:

- A council somewhere in the United States sponsors an event that is open to Girl Scouts throughout the country.
- A traveling Girl Scout group relives the turn of the century in the southern part of the U.S.A. and experiences early Girl Scout tradition by visiting the birthplace of Juliette Low in Savannah, Georgia.
- Girl Scouts of the U.S.A. sponsors an international event and selects U.S.A. Girl Scouts to participate in an international encampment with their sister Girl Scouts/Girl Guides in Europe, Asia, Africa, South America, or some other part of North America.
- You and your troop visit one of WAGGGS's world centers.

Finding Out About Wider Opportunities

Wider opportunities can be sponsored and operated by one or more troops/groups, a neighborhood group, a council, GSUSA, Girl Guide associations, the WAGGGS centers, or by community, national, or international organizations that work with Girl Guides and Girl Scouts.

WIDER OPPORTUNITIES WITHIN THE COUNCIL

There are many ways to find out about local opportunities available to you. Your friends, your leader, and your council are all possible sources of information. There may be notices on bulletin boards or fliers handed out at troop meetings or at school. Sometimes newsletters and special notices are sent out to all registered Cadette and Senior Girl Scouts. Some councils even announce opportunities on radio or cable television. Troop or group members talk about wider opportunities with their friends, classmates, and neighbors.

OPPORTUNITIES WITH NATIONWIDE PARTICIPATION

Each year, Girl Scout councils in many different parts of the country sponsor wider opportunities and invite Girl Scouts from across the United States to apply. These events are called "Wider Opportunities with Nationwide Participation." Girl Scouts of the U.S.A. may also sponsor opportunities at its national centers and elsewhere. Girl Guides/Girl Scouts from other countries are often invited to attend these events. This gives U.S.A. girls the opportunity to meet their international sister Girl Guides/Girl Scouts.

Girl Scouts of the U.S.A. also sponsors international opportunities and selects Cadette and Senior Girl Scouts to participate in international encampments, conferences, community development projects, "home visits," and WAGGGS-sponsored special events in countries around the world.

The locations of opportunities with nationwide participation and the types of activities vary from year to year. Detailed information about these opportunities can be found in *Wider Ops: Girl Scout Wider Opportunities*, a GSUSA annual publication mailed to Girl Scouts ages 12 to 18.

All Cadette and Senior Girl Scouts receive the *Wider Ops* catalog each summer. It provides descriptions of each event and its cost, location, and dates. Special requirements and qualifications along with the number of participants the event can accommodate are noted. Financial aid details, application procedures, and forms are included too.

Who Attends?

Just as there is a great range of wider opportunities, the girls who participate come from a wide range of places—Portland, Oregon; Lagos, Nigeria; Madrid, Spain; Los Angeles, California; Emporia, Kansas; Albany, New York; Rocky Mount, North Carolina; Brandywine, Maryland; and your hometown. They are from rural, suburban, and city areas. They are Black, White, Asian, Hispanic, and Native American. Some speak one language, some two or three. They are Christian, Jewish, Muslim, Buddhist, and other religions as well. Wider opportunities can include your friends and neighbors. Most importantly, though, they can include you!

To make sure that participants have a successful experience, many times the sponsor of a wider opportunity will request that applicants have certain qualifications.

For example, a council sponsoring a large Senior Girl Scout leadership conference might list the following selection criteria.

Participants must:

- be registered Senior Girl Scouts
- be interested in developing leadership skills
- be able to interact with girls from different racial, economic, and ethnic backgrounds
- be able to spend three days away from home
- be in good health

A girl is selected to attend a wider opportunity with nationwide participation by the sponsor of the event. Primarily, girls are selected based on the requirements of the event and the number of participants each event can accommodate. Event sponsors try to select participants from different parts of the country so that everyone attending the event has a chance to meet Girl Scouts from other regions. Sponsors also try to select girls who have never attended a wider opportunity before and girls who are experienced wider opportunity participants. Finally, sponsors make sure that they have girls of various ages and school grades.

The *Wider Ops* catalog provides you with a variety of opportunities from which to choose. To increase your chances of being able to attend, there is a special selection and placement process known as "Operation Second Chance." The application form has spaces for you to list three choices. If you aren't selected to attend your first choice, you could probably be selected to attend your second or third choice, so be sure to fill out the form completely.

Benefits of Wider Opportunities

You, your family, community, troop, group, council, national organization, country, and the World Association of Girl Guides and Girl Scouts—all benefit from wider opportunities.

Through wider opportunities, girls learn first-hand that Girl Scouting extends beyond the boundaries of their own communities to national and international dimensions of the Girl Scout/Girl Guide Movement. These opportunities give girls a chance to find a new world by interacting with their peers from diverse backgrounds, and by enjoying the bonds of friendship and understanding that develop during shared activities. Through these activities, you learn to plan, to assume responsibility, to take initiative, and to work as part of a team. Many experiences may be applied to recognitions such as the Girl Scout Silver Award or the Girl Scout Gold Award (see pages 147–148 and 158–159). For some participants, wider opportunities may even offer the option of earning high school or college credit. Best of all, you'll have fun getting together with others to work on new and different projects.

Let's look at a few comments from girls and their families who have participated in wider opportunities:

"Wider opportunities make you see how strong you are."

"It was a great experience! I learned sign language."

"I loved this experience. Each day held something new."

"It was fun meeting girls from all over the country and some from overseas too!"

"I've grown up a lot and have made some lasting friendships."

"I am more confident now. I can do anything!"

"This was a once-in-a-lifetime experience."

"It made me realize how much of an individual my daughter really is. My daughter's experience with wider opportunities also helped my other children realize the opportunities in life that they could take advantage of too."

"My sister isn't afraid to talk to large groups of people anymore. She really has something to say now."

Girl Guide from Austria: "I learned a lot about American living and the differences between Austria and America: the food, what Americans do, how they live, and how American teenagers are . . . The host families were all so nice to us. We felt we were their own kids, like in our own families."

Girl Guide from Peru: "It was a thoroughly enjoyable trip. I was most impressed by everyone's kindness and willingness to help. I'd love to return, but until I do, I'll continue to exchange letters with all my new Girl Scout friends. Someday I hope they will come and visit me too!"

Girl Scout from the Philippines: "I like North American music a lot. We had lots of fun talking about our school projects, hobbies, friends, and boys. They made me laugh a lot and were very friendly."

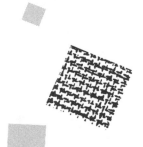

How Much Does It Cost?

The cost of a wider opportunity depends on the type of activities, the accommodations, the length of the event, and the location.

Opportunities within your council are most likely the least expensive. They may be free of charge, or cost anywhere from $5 for meals to $75 or more if overnight accommodations are included.

Opportunities with nationwide participation will probably be more expensive. With the help of your family and your Girl Scout council, you are usually expected to pay the event fee and pay for transportation to and from the event.

These opportunities are announced well in advance so that you can plan ways to earn the money. Part-time jobs like baby-sitting or dog-walking can help your bank account.

Many Girl Scout troops and groups carry out money-earning activities to help girls pay for the cost of their wider opportunity. Before you plan a money-earning activity, you must check with your leader and your council.

Girl Scout councils often have special funds to assist girls who are selected to attend wider opportunities. In addition, "travelships" for wider opportunities with nationwide participation are available through GSUSA. Contact your council for further information on these special scholarships.

Finally, Girl Scouts of the U.S.A. also provides financial help for girls selected to participate in GSUSA-sponsored international opportunities. Information on how these opportunities are financed is found on page 132 of this chapter.

Preparing for a Wider Opportunity

Whether you are planning to attend or sponsor a wider opportunity, knowing exactly what steps to take can help you make the most of your experience. Whether you're planning an opportunity with another troop or attending an international event, the preparation steps are basically the same:

1. *Ask questions*: What are we going to do? When will we do it? For what reason are we doing it? How are we going to do it? Where will the opportunity take place? How long will it be? How will we get there? How much will it cost? How should we get ready? What do we do after it's over?
2. *Know your resources*: Make a list of people, things, materials, pieces of information, and other items you will need to help you prepare for the event. This is your "Needs" list.
3. *Plan strategy*: Identify how you will obtain the things on your "Needs" list. This becomes your "Things to Do" list.
4. *Set priorities*: Put the items on your "Things to Do" list in priority order.
5. *Plan and schedule*: Develop a schedule for beginning and completing the things that you have to do. Keep in mind household, school, and other tasks that you are currently doing so that you can plan a workable timetable. List deadlines that you have to meet. As you complete your tasks, cross them off your list.

Help from Leaders and Former Participants

If you are in a Girl Scout troop or group, you will want to discuss wider opportunities with your leader as well as former participants. Former participants can give you tips on applying, participating, and sharing your experience after it's over. Your leader can give you guidelines for attending different opportunities, perhaps arranging for you to attend a special workshop for prospective wider opportunity participants. Councils sometimes sponsor these workshops in which girls are given tips on filling out application forms and obtaining references, participate in games that introduce them to new and different situations, role-play skits on being away from home or being interviewed by a girl/adult selection panel, plan money-earning projects, have discussions on representing GSUSA, research a wider opportunity, organize themselves to attend, and communicate their experiences to others.

Here are some other activities that can help you and your troop to learn more about wider opportunities:

1. Organize a wider opportunity information day for your troop/group and invite family members to attend. Collect information on wider opportunities and invite former wider opportunities participants to share the highlights of their experiences.
2. Interview former wider opportunities participants, then write a newsletter for your troop and/or neighborhood telling what you have learned from the interviews.
3. Design posters and fliers that would advertise a wider opportunity offered by your group, neighborhood, council, or even an event listed in *Wider Ops*.

Applying for an Opportunity with Nationwide Participation

Filling out an application form is an important step in the selection process. Be sure to follow instructions and fill out the form completely and as neatly as possible. Parents, family members, Girl Scout leaders, and teachers can all be a great help, especially in obtaining references about your qualifications.

Once you've completed an application, make a copy of it. You can refer to it when completing future applications or when applying for other events.

Girls are usually interviewed by their council as part of the process of applying for a wider opportunity. This is an important step in helping others to know you. It's one way to make certain the right person is selected for the right event.

When you are applying for a wider opportunity, remember that both your Girl Scout and non-Girl Scout experiences and skills count, no matter how large or small they seem to you. Your ability to handle yourself away from home and with people from different backgrounds is extremely important as well as your interest in the opportunity and the skills you can bring to the event.

International Opportunities

Each year, Girl Scouts of the U.S.A. receives invitations from Girl Guides and Girl Scouts around the world to send girls and adults to special events in their countries. The invitations can be for national or international encampments, community service projects, home visits, or events at the world centers.

When you apply for an international opportunity, you are not applying for a special event in a specific place. If and when you are selected, you will be given full information about the location and nature of the international wider opportunity, and you'll have time to prepare for your trip.

Participants in international opportunities are selected because they demonstrate an interest in international events; emotional maturity; flexibility in coping with unexpected situations; ability to deal with group living; and acceptance of cultural and ethnic differences. A council interview, council endorsement of your application form, and two references are also required. A national task group meets each year to make the selections for international opportunities.

Juliette Low World Friendship Fund

The costs of international opportunities vary greatly, depending on where the events take place. The Juliette Low World Friendship Fund helps to meet some of the costs for all participants in GSUSA-sponsored international opportunites. A girl attending an event in a faraway country such as India pays the same as a girl attending an event in Mexico. Financial assistance from the fund is also available to girls who need help with their share of the costs. Juliette Low believed in friendship among all girls. The fund makes this possible. Through the contributions of Girl Scouts throughout the country, it helps to send U.S.A. Girl Scouts to international events and to bring girls from WAGGGS member countries to U.S.A. events.

Each year Girl Scout troops/groups, neighborhoods, and councils collect moneys for the Juliette Low World Friendship Fund. The money is sent to Girl Scouts of the U.S.A. to be used for international opportunities and for other international projects.

Other International Wider Opportunities in Girl Scouting

INTERNATIONAL POST BOX

Girl Scouts who are 11 to 17 years old can request a pen pal from Girl Scouts of the U.S.A. by getting a special form from their Girl Scout councils. You must use this form; otherwise, your request will not be considered. Fill out the form very neatly, in ink, and send it to Girl Scout national headquarters. (The address is on the form.) Staff members at national headquarters will then try to link you with a pen pal in one of the areas of the world that you request. However, you will have to be patient. Whether or not you will get a pen pal depends on how many other U.S.A. Girl Scouts are asking for pen pals from the same areas, and how many girls from those areas want pen pals here. Sometimes it just isn't possible to find pen pals for everyone. If you are one of the lucky girls who does get a pen pal, it will still take at least six months; but the wait will be worth it, because many Girl Scout/Girl Guide pen pals correspond for years and become life-long friends.

TRAVELING TROOPS, GROUPS, AND INDIVIDUALS

Many Cadette and Senior Girl Scouts individually and in troops and groups have visited Our Cabaña (Cuernavaca, Mexico), Pax Lodge (London, England), Our Chalet (Adelboden, Switzerland), and Sangam (Pune, India). All of the world centers have their doors open welcoming traveling Girl Scouts and Girl Guides. Girls may attend sessions at the center or may visit at any time during the year when regular meetings or sessions are not in progress there. Such visits should, of course, be planned well in advance.

Here's what one former Girl Scout troop did before traveling to Our Chalet.

Mrs. Prado's troop indicated to her that they wanted to travel to Our Chalet. It sounded like a good idea so the troop investigated how to do this. Troop #84 found out through their council the following information:

■ As soon as there is an interest in traveling outside the United States, leaders and girls should inform the council and get permission to plan the trip.

■ The chapter entitled "Planning Trips with Girl Scouts," in *Safety-Wise*, contains the basic information on how to plan such a trip.

■ The procedures for traveling abroad, including visiting, obtaining accommodations, and taking part in current activities at a world center or a Girl Scout/Girl Guide headquarters, can be obtained through the council and/or through the Program Group, GSUSA.

■ The troop should *not* directly contact Girl Guide/Girl Scout offices in other countries for information or for help with travel plans. It is the policy of the World Association of Girl Guides and Girl Scouts that individual members do not write to national organizations other than their own.

The procedures developed by the World Association help to protect the health, safety, security, and interest of travelers and hosts. A trip abroad is the culmination of one to three years of serious planning and hard work by girls and leaders. When Cadette or Senior Girl Scouts begin to dream about traveling, they should begin to seek help.

Troop #84 obtained information on procedures, guidelines, and preparation from their council and from GSUSA. They held a troop meeting and decided that they would plan to go to Our Chalet in two years, preferably in July. So Mrs. Prado and the girls began to make all kinds of preparation plans, from researching the climate in Switzerland in July, to carrying out money-earning activities, to becoming travel- and culture-wise. Planning to attend two years in advance gave them plenty of time to prepare. Having the support and advice of their leader, council, and GSUSA made a lot of sense, and helped turn the troop's plans into a dream come true.

Here are some suggested activities to help prepare you for international events:

1. On a map, pinpoint the WAGGGS member countries, Girl Scout national centers, and world centers.
2. Plan a people awareness day. Invite people from different ethnic, religious, and cultural backgrounds to share their heritage and culture.
3. Listen to music from other countries or see a foreign film.
4. Cook international dishes.
5. Begin to learn a foreign language.
6. Conduct global issues workshops with other members of your troop or group. Learn about world hunger, freedom struggles, nuclear disarmament, environmental abuse, and other subjects.
7. Design a game about American history and government (either a board game or a nonboard game).

Widening Circles: A Reference Chart on the Basics of Wider Opportunities

On the facing page you will find a reference chart called "Widening Circles." What better way to say, "Look wide and when you think you're looking wide, look wider still."

Planning Your Own Wider Opportunity

You, too, can sponsor a wider opportunity. You can start with your own troop right in your own backyard. Think of the enjoyment you and your troop would get from planning and inviting other Girl Scouts and non-Girl Scouts to a special wider opportunity.

Before starting to plan a wider opportunity, become familiar with the key elements for designing one. Wider opportunities should be designed to reflect the values that Girl Scouting can offer. They should:

■ Meet the needs of girls.
■ Follow the basic principles of Girl Scouting.
■ Relate to issues of today's world.
■ Contribute to community development.
■ Develop a sense of belonging to a worldwide movement: the World Association of Girl Guides and Girl Scouts (WAGGGS).
■ Inspire girls to continue their involvement in the Movement.
■ Provide girls with opportunities for planning and decision-making.
■ Provide girls with opportunities for meeting new people, seeing new places, trying new activities, and working with adults.

WIDENING CIRCLES
Girl Scout Experiences Beyond the Troop Setting

Wider Opportunities Within the Council

Attended by: girls within the council, and sometimes girls from neighboring councils.

Sponsored by: a troop, a neighborhood, or the council. Examples: troop trips, intertroop projects, ceremonies, neighborhood events, service projects, courses (such as first aid, arts, skating), interest group, double dutch, weekend events, troop camp, core camp, summer camp, traveling troops (within the United States).

Wider Opportunities with Nationwide Participation

Attended by: girls nationwide, and sometimes international participants.

Sponsored by: a council in camps, colleges, conference centers. Examples: high-adventure outdoor events, service/career exploration events, arts events, events focusing on current affairs or global issues.

At Juliette Gordon Low Center: wider opportunities for individuals and for troops.

At Edith Macy Conference Center: opportunities for individuals.

Other opportunities: program conferences, other conferences on contemporary issues.

International Wider Opportunities

Attended by: U.S.A. Girl Scouts and Girl Scouts/Girl Guides.

Sponsored by: a troop, a neighborhood, or a council. Examples: trips abroad, trips to WAGGGS world centers (Our Cabaña, Our Chalet, Sangam, Pax Lodge).

Sponsored by: GSUSA (financed by the Juliette Low World Friendship Fund). Examples: international events in the U.S.A., delegations to international encampments, conferences, community development projects, "home visits," WAGGGS-sponsored special events, international visitors to councils in special "council-designed" projects, international participants in council-sponsored wider opportunities with nationwide participation, international participants in GSUSA-sponsored events.

PLANNING THE OPPORTUNITY—STEP BY STEP

Planning an event could be called the challenge of "how to think of everything." The details of planning can seem endless, but organizing in advance will simplify your work. Try to be as thorough as possible and predict your needs, but be prepared to add or subtract items as you go along.

You can make your path more manageable by dividing it into stages, each of which can stand on its own. By making your time and energy commitment reasonable, you will make your project more enjoyable. Your leader can help you with allotting time to your best advantage.

Stage 1: Decide on the Wider Opportunity You Would Like to Do

■ You and your group decide that you want to hold a wider opportunity.
■ Discuss and make a list of about six possible activities or events that you might want to do.
■ Select two or three major choices from the list. For each of the choices, consider:

Its purpose.
Its potential benefits.
The need for this kind of opportunity in your troop, neighborhood, or community.
The key elements of a Girl Scout wider opportunity.
The number of participants and whom to invite.
The date, time, and length of the opportunity.
Whether this is the right time of year to have this particular kind of activity.
Other activities that may be going on at the same time as yours.
Personal, school, household, and other obligations that could possibly restrict your group from holding the event.
Health and safety factors, the necessary permissions from your Girl Scout council and community organizations, etc.
The cost. (Think of costs for food, location rental, transportation, equipment, supplies, etc.)
Who will become project officers and what their responsibilities will be (director, assistant director, secretary, treasurer).
Adult consultants, resources needed, etc.

After weighing the strengths and weaknesses of the two or three activities or events that you have selected, take a vote on them to decide which one is best to do.

Stage 2: Define the Opportunity

Discuss, plan, and list the following:

■ Purpose of the event.
■ Desired results (what you want participants to get out of it).
■ Agenda or itinerary.

- Dates and times (include several as backup).
- Participants (the number of people expected to attend, whom to invite).
- Qualifications or requirements for participation.
- Name, theme, or focus.
- Project officers.
- Names, addresses, and telephone numbers of individuals who will serve as contact people.

The beginning of your list might look like this if your troop decided to sponsor a visit to a local radio station.

Name of event: Visit to WKYS, a local radio station

Date: Saturday, October 24. (Backup dates: Saturday, November 7 or Saturday, November 14.)

Time: 2:00–5:00 P.M. (Backup time: 10:00 A.M.–1:00 P.M.)

Purpose: To observe the operation of a radio station. To become familiar with the equipment and types of jobs needed to operate one.

Stage 3: Identify Your Needs and Resources

- Make a list of everything you will need in order to complete your activity. Think of what you will need before, during, and after the event.

    The list may include advice, supplies, equipment, activity ideas, location/site, books, training, transportation, people, food, publicity, work space, budget, etc.
- Now make a list of all of the individual people, organizations, materials, supplies, and other things that you have access to, or may already have available to help meet your needs. These are your resources.

    Resource people are very valuable. They can help to decrease the cost of the project, evenly divide or decrease the workload, enrich the content, and increase the visibility and recognition of your event. They can help the event to run smoothly.

    Your family and community can become resources for obtaining people, places, and things. Do you have family members who can serve as trainers or guest speakers, provide food or equipment, or help out in some other way?

    Other possible resources are community organizations, international students, teachers, health officials, government officials, business persons, books, magazines, newspapers, movies, television/radio programs, museums, libraries, stores.

Your wider opportunity needs and resource list might look something like the one on the next page if your group has decided to conduct a sports day for Daisy and Brownie Girl Scouts.

Sports Day for Daisy and Brownie Girl Scouts

Needs	Resources
1. Project description	Your troop or group leader.
2. Advice on holding a Girl Scout wider opportunity	Leader, council, *Safety-Wise*, this *Cadette and Senior Girl Scout Handbook*, *Cadette and Senior Girl Scouts Leaders' Guide*, other girls who have held wider opportunities.
3. Program activities	*Brownie Girl Scout Handbook*, *Daisy Girl Scouts Leaders' Guide*, *Brownie Girl Scouts Leaders' Guide*. Films, books, and ideas from Daisy and Brownie Girl Scouts, friends, family, teachers, leaders, libraries, and sports groups.
4. Equipment and supplies	Physical education teachers, coaches, community sports and recreation groups, local council.
5. People to work on Sports Day (including teachers and guest speakers)	Friends in and out of Girl Scouting, coaches, teachers, family, community sports and recreation people.
6. Location/site	School, council, community center, local park service.
7. Health, safety, and security regulations	*Safety-Wise*, leader, council, sports and recreation staff, physical education teacher, coach, location/site director, school nurse, first aid instructors.
8. Promotion and publicity	Local radio stations, newspapers, stores, schools, local colleges and universities, public library, leader, council media people.
9. Work space	Home, parent's place of work, community center, civic organizations, religious organizations, public library, Girl Scout council, local museum, meeting rooms.
10. Refreshments	Family, friends, neighbors, community organizations, local stores.
11. Transportation	Family, friends, leader, council, public transportation.
12. Budget	Leader and all other resources listed above.

Stage 4: List Areas of Responsibility. Who Will Be Responsible for Them? What Needs to Be Done in Each Area?

For each area of responsibility, a planning team can be formed. Planning teams should get together to think of everything that needs to be done in their area from the beginning to the end of the project. All teams must regularly communicate with one another. Your project officers will help you to do this.

For instance, the location/site planning team's main responsibility might be to acquire an appropriate place for the event. They may have to look at different places to see if there are tables, chairs, electrical outlets, restrooms, telephones, a kitchen, a refrigerator. They might have to see if the area is accessible, healthy, and safe, then get a site permit and reserve the area. Members of this team would check with the health and safety team to see what the Girl Scout health and safety requirements are. They would need to let the transportation, program, and equipment teams know about the site's special regulations, parking facilities, space, equipment, and supplies. They would also need to let the food/refreshments team know if the site has a refrigerator. What else might they need to report? To whom?

Try these activities to help you learn about operating your own wider opportunity:

1. Imagine that your troop and another troop are planning to create a community flower garden. Complete the chart below:

Needs	Resources	Areas of Responsibility
_____	_____	_____
_____	_____	_____
_____	_____	_____
_____	_____	_____
_____	_____	_____
_____	_____	_____

2. List what you think needs to be done in one of the areas of responsibility listed above.
3. Create a community resource file. List the names, addresses, and phone numbers of community organizations, libraries, schools, museums, religious institutions, stores, etc., that may be able to help you.

Stage 5: Develop a Work Schedule

Each planning team should develop a realistic plan for beginning and completing the things that it needs to do. Put your list in order of priorities. Ask your leader to assist you.

The project officers should collect work schedules from each planning team and set up planning meetings based on each group's schedule. They should also draw up an overall work chart to help keep track of when each task is to be done and who is to do it.

Stage 6: Do the Activity: All Set and Ready to Go!

Welcome and greet participants, staff, and resource people with a smile. Be pleasant and helpful.

All workers should be at their assigned areas in advance and ready to go. Check with project officers and other team members periodically for any last-minute instructions or changes. Have a good time!

Stage 7: Evaluate and Follow Up

- Return materials.
- Replenish depleted supplies.
- Replace any damaged materials.
- Evaluate the project—participants and project staff should both evaluate the wider opportunity.
- Make recommendations for the future.
- Send out thank-you notes and letters of appreciation.

Your records will help you evaluate the success of your program. As you look back, with the specifics in front of you, you can find ways to improve your plan. By recognizing weak spots, you can be sure of a better experience next time around.

Reaching Wider Still

Wider opportunities can be challenging and fun. They can place you in the center of a series of widening circles, whirling you from the inner circles of your dreams to the outer circles of the world. As you gather in your troop or group to talk about wider opportunities, remember you can "reach wide" in as many directions as you like and as often as you like. Wider opportunities can be the start of something big for you!

9

RECOGNITIONS FOR CADETTE AND SENIOR GIRL SCOUTS

As a Cadette or Senior Girl Scout you have the opportunity to earn recognition for many of your efforts. This chapter describes the recognitions available to you in your work in Cadette and Senior Girl Scouting.

As you review all the material in this book, you will see that there is a great assortment of things to do. Each recognition has a specific set of requirements. When these are completed, you are entitled to receive the outward symbol of accomplishment. This may be a patch, a badge, or a pin. Many activities may be completed alone and many are best suited to working in a group. It will be important for you to follow through on your decision-making skills and chart a plan best suited to your needs. Note that the key to successful Girl Scout work is a partnership with an adult.

Remember that your experiences and what you have learned are most important. The patch, pin, or badge is just a symbol of your work. It is quality, not quantity, that matters.

General Guidelines for Completing Requirements

The work in completing a recognition varies greatly from individual to individual, but the following general guidelines will be helpful:

1. Work with an adult. This may not always be the same person. It may be a troop leader or assistant leader, an adviser, a group coordinator, or a program consultant; it may at times even be a member of your family. The adult partner will give you guidance and assistance in completing the work. She or he should initial the completed requirements.

2. Keep a record of your work. This work may be helpful for future endeavors such as school admissions, job applications, or work on other Girl Scout recognitions. You may use this handbook or design your own personal record-keeping system that may include written

documentation, oral presentations, tape or video recordings, exhibits, photographs, etc.

3. The same work completed for one recognition requirement may not also be counted for other recognition requirements. However, you may build upon a particular activity and do additional work so that the effort can be expanded for more than one requirement. For example, the work on designing a career fair to earn the Career Exploration pin may not also be used to earn the Career Exploration interest project patch. However, you could plan to do extra related work after the career fair is over and apply that to the interest project.

4. Remember the Girl Scout Promise and Law in all that you do. This will guide you in doing your best work possible. Shortcuts and bending rules not only defeat the learning potential of your work, but they are not in keeping with the meaning of your Girl Scout efforts.

Recognitions for Cadette
Girl Scouts

TAN BADGES

Girl Scout Badges and Signs contains a selection of badges with a tan background. Girl Scout badges are designed to build skills and increase your proficiency in a particular area. Although these badges were primarily designed for the Junior Girl Scout, the tan badges demand a higher level of work and commitment than those with green backgrounds and may be earned by Cadette Girl Scouts.

CADETTE GIRL SCOUT LEADERSHIP AWARD

The Cadette Girl Scout Leadership Award calls for you to participate in experiences that build leadership skills. You earn this recognition by completing the starred requirements:

✱ Read the "Leadership and Groups" chapter in this handbook.

✱ Complete the activities dealing with leadership roles and leadership qualities on page 43 in this handbook.

Then put your leadership skills into action in the basic leadership situations described below. Your work should total a minimum of 25 hours on two or more of the leadership activities listed. At least three hours must be spent on each activity. For example, if you log 25 hours on one weekend camping trip, you will have to complete an additional leadership activity at another time for at least three hours. Keep a log of your experiences. The record should be brief and should include a short self-evaluation of your leadership.

Serve a term as an officer in a group. (This may be in Girl Scouting or with school, church, recreation groups, etc.)

Assist in the leadership of a group of younger children. (This may be in a variety of settings—troop, interest group, camp, etc.)

Serve as a program aide. See page 57 in this handbook.

Take charge of planning a major trip or special event for your group.

Complete a long-range planning calendar for your troop or group. Refer to pages 52–53 in this handbook for helpful information.

Work with an adult who is in a leadership position. Discuss the leadership skills she uses in her job and how your experiences can help you build these skills.

FROM DREAMS TO REALITY ACTIVITIES PATCH

To earn the From Dreams to Reality activities patch, you must complete career exploration activities as described below. Do the one starred requirement and then select four more activities from the options that follow.

✳Read the "From Dreams to Reality: Career Exploration" chapter in this handbook. Take the career interests test on pages 82–83.

Complete the career abilities chart on page 84.

Find out about at least five of the careers listed on page 88. Be sure to find out such information as type of training needed and average salary range.

Play the "career creation" game on pages 89–90.

Find out about two women employed in fields in which women are not the majority.

Interview at least three different working women in your community. Find out how they came to be in their current positions and what their future hopes and dreams might be.

Collect several want ads for at least three different types of positions that you are interested in learning about. Use pages 100–101 to help you in understanding common abbreviations. Compare the ads to get a general profile of each position.

CADETTE GIRL SCOUT CHALLENGE

As a Girl Scout, you are challenged to be the best possible person you can be. This involves knowing yourself, relating well to other people, understanding and acting upon your values, and contributing to the well-being of your community.

The Cadette Girl Scout Challenge has five sections. Each has a "prep" (short for "preparation step") that prepares you for the challenge activities that follow.

To earn the Challenge, complete each of the five sections. These may be done in any order, but it is recommended that you follow them in the sequence listed. You may work on several at one time or do each of them separately. They may be done with others in your troop, or you may work on them alone. Take time to discuss each section with your leader or adult partner.

After you have completed each prep, you are ready to put what you have discovered about yourself and others to work.

Section 1: Knowing Myself Better

Prep Read the "Personal Development" chapter in this handbook.

Challenge Select one of the following activities, or design one of your own that helps you to know yourself better.

Complete the "Take a Look at Yourself" and "Positive Thinking" activities on pages 19 and 22 in this handbook.

Make a list of qualities you value in a friend. Mark those qualities you already possess. From the rest of the list, choose one or two qualities you would like to have. Over a three- to four-week period, make every effort to make these qualities your own.

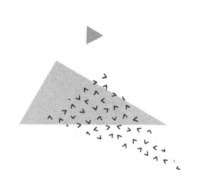

Try something new, a new skill or activity. Find out who could help you in gaining the new skill and seek out their help. Spend at least five hours trying something new to you.

Try two or more activities in the Fashion/Fitness/Makeup interest project (see *Cadette and Senior Girl Scout Interest Projects*) to change or improve your overall appearance.

Section 2: Relating to Others Better

Prep Read the "Relationships" chapter in this handbook.

Challenge Do one of the activities below, or design your own activity in which skills in relating to other people are important.

Complete either the "Family Symbol" activity or the "Family Timeline" activity, both on page 28 in this handbook.

Complete the "Friendly Networks" activity on page 31 in this handbook.

Read the "Peer Pressure" section on pages 34–36 in this handbook. Identify and evaluate several instances in which you were negatively and positively affected by peer pressure.

Plan and carry out an outing or party for family, hospital patients, senior citizens, or a group in your community.

Plan and carry out a coed event, such as a day of sports or backpacking, a debate, or a party. Include boys on the planning committee.

Section 3: Developing Values for Living

Prep Read the following sections in this handbook: "Values" (pages 24–26) and "Citizen of the World" (pages 105–124).

Challenge Do at least one of the following activities.

Complete all the activities in the prejudice and discrimination sections of the "Citizen of the World" chapter (pages 108–111).

Do all the activities in the values section of the "Personal Development" chapter (pages 24–26).

Take an active part in planning and carrying out a Girl Scouts' Own, which demonstrates the ways the Girl Scout Promise and Law can help you to show your feelings about serving God and your country and about your pledge to be a good citizen. (See "Ceremonies" section, pages 14–15, for further information.)

Think of at least one value you have that you would like to strengthen. Develop a short-range plan that will enable you to act upon this value.

Section 4: Contributing to your Community

Prep   You can give something of yourself and make an impact on your community. "Community" is used in a very broad way and includes Girl Scouting. Review the "Citizen of the World" chapter to help you decide what might be done and how to get started.

Challenge   Decide on an activity that you can do to benefit your community. You may select from the following idea list or complete an activity of your own.

Organize a children's sports day, assist at a community New Games festival, or assist at a Special Olympics (for persons with disabilities).

Assist as a literacy volunteer; help with programs for refugee peoples; help spread the word about getting out to vote, immunization, food stamps, etc.

Serve as an audiovisual assistant in your school, troop, council, house of worship; be a math or science tutor.

Teach crafts to children, work on an art project with senior citizens, provide arts activities in a hospital or residential school.

Demonstrate water safety for younger girls, help repair and maintain your council's small craft, help on a community clean water project.

Section 5: Knowing About Girl Scouting

Prep   Read the "About Girl Scouting" chapter in this handbook.

Challenge   Select one of the following activities or design one of your own that shows you have knowledge of Girl Scouting, its purpose, and its history.

Design an activity that will help others know about the Girl Scout Movement and WAGGGS.

Using *The Wide World of Girl Guiding and Girl Scouting* (GSUSA Cat. No. 19-713, 1980) as a model, prepare a booklet or presentation for younger girls on at least two other countries that are members of the World Association. *Trefoil Round the World* (WAGGGS, Cat. No. 23-962, revised 1986) is a handy reference on the history of Girl Scouting and Girl Guiding.

Write a biography, a series of poems or songs, a fictionalized account, a play, or choreograph a dance on Juliette Gordon Low and/or other important people in the history of the Girl Scout Movement.

Follow a council staff member, camp staff person, or volunteer for at least several hours. Assist her as much as possible and learn about her work and about Girl Scouting as a profession or outside activity.

Learn about the ways to volunteer in Girl Scouting.

Help your council recruit new members in Girl Scouting.

Do volunteer work at your Girl Scout council office for at least several hours, assisting with the regular work or with a special project.

When you have completed all five sections of the Cadette Girl Scout Challenge, ask yourself these questions:

> What did you learn about yourself?
>
> In what way(s) did your Challenge work have an impact on others?
>
> In what way(s) did you use your talents?
>
> How do your accomplishments relate to the ideals of Girl Scouting?
>
> How would you improve what you did?
>
> What do the things you learned through this Challenge mean for you in the future?

GIRL SCOUT SILVER AWARD

The Girl Scout Silver Award recognizes your efforts in a wide range of Girl Scout experiences and your commitment to working to better your life and the lives of others. There are five requirements for this award. You should work closely with your adult partners in the completion of all the requirements. The first four call upon you to build your skills, explore career possibilities, increase your leadership skills, and make a commitment to improving yourself. These requirements may be done in any order but must be completed before you work on the fifth requirement, the Girl Scout Silver Award project.

Requirements

Requirements started prior to Cadette Girl Scouting may not be applied toward this award.

1. Earn three interest project patches.
2. Earn the From Dreams to Reality activities patch outlined on page 144.
   OR
   Earn the Career Exploration interest project patch.
3. Earn the Cadette Girl Scout Leadership Award (pages 143–144).
   OR
   Earn the Leadership interest project patch.
4. Earn the Cadette Girl Scout Challenge (pages 144–147).
5. Design and carry out a Girl Scout Silver Award project.

This project builds upon your accomplishments in Girl Scouting. Your project is your personal action plan for helping others. It is your opportunity to use all that you have learned in the first four requirements to benefit others. The project has four steps. As you complete each step, fill in the report form on pages 163–164.

Step 1 Decide what talents and abilities you would like to put into action through a project that will improve the lives of others.

Step 2 Think about your values, what you care about, and how you'd like to make something better. Develop a plan that will use your personal strengths to help others. This may involve school, the community, a religious group, or Girl Scouting.

Step 3 Identify the people with whom you will work: those who will help and guide you, those who will work with you, those whom you hope to help.

Step 4 Carry out your plan. This final step of your project should total at least seven hours. This may be all on one day or divided into segments. When you have completed your project, write a brief evaluation.

BRIDGE TO SENIOR GIRL SCOUTS PATCH

Moving from one Girl Scout age level to the next is called bridging. When you complete each of the eight bridging steps, you will be entitled to receive the Bridge to Senior Girl Scouts patch.

1. Find out about all the age levels in Girl Scouting. Interview at least two former or current Senior Girl Scouts to find out what they do as part of their Girl Scout activities.
2. Read the section on recognitions for Senior Girl Scouts (see pages 152–160).
3. Do something with a Senior Girl Scout.
4. Help others learn about Cadette and/or Senior Girl Scouting.
5. Find out about Leader-in-Training and Counselor-in-Training opportunities available in your area and review a *Wider Ops* catalog to see what opportunities are open to Senior Girl Scouts only.
6. Complete a leadership activity with a group of younger Girl Scouts.
7. Plan your bridging ceremony.
8. Plan and do a summer Girl Scout activity.

OTHER RECOGNITIONS

Recognitions that can be earned by both Cadette and Senior Girl Scouts are described in the following section.

Recognitions for Cadette and Senior Girl Scouts

INTEREST PROJECT PATCHES

Cadette as well as Senior Girl Scouts may increase their skills and gain recognition for their proficiency in a wide range of subjects. Interest projects are similar to Girl Scout badges but require a higher level of skill and understanding.

The total range of interest projects as well as information on designing your own may be found in *Cadette and Senior Girl Scout Interest Projects*.

RELIGIOUS RECOGNITIONS FOR CADETTE AND SENIOR GIRL SCOUTS

Through Girl Scouting, each girl is encouraged to become a stronger member of her own religious group. To help girls grow in this area, the religious recognition programs listed here have been developed by and are administered by the religious groups themselves. The pins presented by each religious group may be worn on the Girl Scout uniform.

The religious recognition programs listed here are available nationwide. There are also many religious recognition programs that have been developed by individual religious groups for local use. Check with your local clergy or youth minister for information on such programs in your area.

For Girls of the Roman Catholic Faith

The Marian Medal, a program for girls ages 12–15, involves participants in increasing their understanding of Mary as a model of openness and spirituality, a woman of the church. For further information, talk to your parish priest or youth minister, or get in touch with your Roman Catholic Diocesan Youth Director or Girl Scout Chaplain, or write to: National Federation for Catholic Youth Ministry, 3900-A Harewood Road, N.E., Washington, D.C. 20017, Attn: Orders Clerk.

For Girls of the Jewish Faith

The Menorah Award, for girls ages 11–17, emphasizes understanding of a girl's Jewish heritage through daily home observances, Sabbath and holiday observances, study of the Bible and Jewish history, and learning about the Jewish community in the United States and worldwide. This program was developed and is administered by the National Jewish Girl Scout Committee of the Synagogue Council of America, 327 Lexington Avenue, New York, N.Y. 10016.

For Girls of the Reorganized Church of Jesus Christ of the Latter Day Saints

The World Community series has programs that lead a girl through interesting growing experiences in all the important aspects of life: Liahona, for ages 11–14; Exploring My Life and World, for ages 15–18. The Christian Education Commission, The Auditorium, P.O. Box 1059, Independence, Mo. 64051 administers the programs.

For Girls of the Eastern Orthodox Faith

Alpha Omega, for girls ages 11 and older, emphasizes a girl's life and actions as an Orthodox Christian, the work and organization of her parish church, and service projects for the church. Orthodox Scouting Commission, 27-09 Crescent Street, Long Island City, N.Y. 11102 administers the program.

For Girls of the Protestant and Independent Churches

God and Church, for grades 6–9, provides a girl with an opportunity to know her pastor and counselor better, to understand her church's structure and objectives, and to participate in services and projects that will give her a better understanding of the mission of her church. God and Life, for grades 10 and up, is a program in which young adults, working with their pastor or counselor, will concern themselves with their faith and how they relate to their church, their family, their community, and their country.

These programs, which are part of the God and Country series, were developed and are administered by Programs of Religious Activities with Youth (P.R.A.Y.), P.O. Box 6900, St. Louis, Mo. 63123.

For Girls of the Lutheran Faith

God-Home-Country, for girls ages 12 and older, is designed to motivate girls to be active participants in all aspects of their church's program and to think deeply about participation in congregational and community life in response to God's love leading them to faith. Programs of Religious Activities with Youth (P.R.A.Y.), Box 6900, St. Louis, Mo. 63123.

For Girls of the Buddhist Faith

The Padma Award, a four-part program with activities for Brownie, Junior, Cadette, and Senior Girl Scouts, is designed to help girls put into practice the ideals of the Buddhist faith and of the Girl Scout Promise and Law. National Buddhist Committee on Scouting, Buddhist Churches of America, 1710 Octavia Street, San Francisco, Calif. 94109 administers the program.

For Girls Who Are Unitarian Universalists

Religion in Life, developed by the Unitarian Universalist Association for Junior, Cadette, and Senior Girl Scouts, is a program of reading, thought, discussion, and action in Unitarian Universalist principles and action. The program is administered by the Unitarian Universalist Association, Distribution Center, 25 Beacon Street, Boston, Mass. 02108.

For Girls of The Church of Jesus Christ of Latter-day Saints

The Young Women's organization of the Church of Jesus Christ of Latter-day Saints recommends that girls ages 12–18 meet the requirements of the

My Personal Progress program. For each year that a girl achieves her set goals in each of six areas, she will receive a certificate. Continuing these same requirements would help a girl to become eligible to apply for the Young Womanhood Recognition certificate and medallion at age 17. The medallion that a girl earns may be worn on her Girl Scout uniform. The program is administered by The Church of Jesus Christ of Latter-day Saints, 1999 West 1700 South, Salt Lake City, Utah 84104.

For Girls of the Unity Church

Light of God for girls ages 11–13 is designed to give young people in Unity a practical method for achieving a basic spiritual understanding of the truths taught by Unity and is designed to support and recognize youth for their achievement, in the presence of the church body.

The Filmore Youth Award for girls ages 14–17 gives young adults in Unity the opportunity to achieve a deeper understanding of the truths taught by Unity and a practical method of practicing them.

Both of the above recognitions were developed and are administered by the Association of Unity Churches, P.O. Box 610, Lee's Summit, Mo. 64063.

For Girls Who Are Christian Scientists

The God and Country program, for Cadette and Senior Girl Scouts in grades 6–10, is designed to bring to Girl Scouting activities a greater sense of serving mankind through living the teachings of Christian Science. The program is administered by the First Church of Christ, Scientist, Sunday School Activities, A142 Christian Science Center, Boston, Mass. 02115.

AMERICAN INDIAN YOUTH CERTIFICATE AND AWARD

Any registered Girl Scout age 12 through 17 may earn an American Indian Youth Certificate and attend the annual American Indian Girl Scouting/ Boy Scouting Seminar. Also, participants who are of American Indian heritage may compete for the annual American Indian Youth Award. Note that the sponsors periodically make changes in the requirements for the certificate and award. Up-to-date information is available, free of charge, from Girl Scout national headquarters. (Order *American Indian Youth Certificate and Award*, FM No. 40-155-020, from Free Materials, Girl Scouts of the U.S.A., 830 Third Avenue, New York, N.Y. 10022.)

LEADER-IN-TRAINING AND COUNSELOR-IN-TRAINING PROJECT PINS

Leader-in-Training (LIT) and Counselor-in-Training (CIT) courses provide excellent ways for Girl Scouts 14 years and older to gain valuable leadership skills while giving service to their councils. The two courses may be given separately or combined in a coordinated and accelerated training experience.

Each council develops courses to meet the unique needs of the girls it serves. When you have completed a council LIT and/or CIT training course, you will be entitled to receive a pin that signifies you are an LIT or a CIT. Your work as an LIT or a CIT may be applied to recognitions listed in this chapter.

See pages 57–60 for further information.

SERVICE TRAINING BARS

Girl Scout service training is an apprenticeship program where you learn specific skills to help you give volunteer service in your community. The skills you develop in the service training sessions not only help you in your volunteer work now but can be a way to gain valuable knowledge that will help you in your future work. Volunteer service training sessions may be concentrated in one of the worlds of interest or may relate to the general world of Girl Scouting.

The service training is set up in conjunction with your council. Often another agency or organization, or other community resources in your area, are partners with your council in providing the training. To find out what service training sessions are available at the present time, check with your Girl Scout council. Once you have discussed and chosen a project with your leader and council, the necessary arrangements with the cooperating agency or organization will be made.

The requirements for a Service Training bar are that you:

■ Be a registered Girl Scout.
■ Meet the age and/or grade requirements established by your council and/or the service organization.
■ Complete the required training course.
■ Make a commitment to give a minimum of 25 hours of service following training.

When you complete your service training, you will be eligible for a Service Training bar, which may be worn on your Girl Scout uniform when you are giving service. One or more Service Training bars can be earned in Girl Scouting and in each of the five worlds of interest.

Recognitions for Senior Girl Scouts

SENIOR GIRL SCOUT LEADERSHIP AWARD

The Senior Girl Scout Leadership Award builds on your previous leadership experiences. The purpose is to deepen and broaden your skills as a leader. To earn this award, you must complete the starred requirement and apply what you have learned to leadership activities as noted below.

✳ Read or reread the chapter on "Leadership and Groups" and do the activities on pages 43, 47, and 49.

Log at least 30 hours in two or more of the following activities. If you spend 30 or more hours on only one of the options below, you must still work on a second activity option for a minimum of three hours. The experiences may be in or outside of Girl Scouting.

Serve a term as an officer in a group.

Assist in the leadership of a group of younger children. (This may be in a variety of settings—troop, interest group, day care center, camp, etc.)

Plan and give a public presentation. It may be a talk, panel, or dramatization as outlined on pages 48–49 in this handbook.

Serve in a leadership capacity for your council. This may be as a board member, council committee member, delegate to the National Council, planning board member, or other function designated by your council.

Work with an adult who is in a leadership position with children or adults.

CAREER EXPLORATION PIN

To earn the Career Exploration pin, you must complete the starred requirements and at least one of the other options listed.

✴Read or reread the "From Dreams to Reality" chapter in this handbook.

✴Write your own résumé. Follow the guidelines on pages 102–103.

Option 1: Plan a Career Fair

Share career information with your friends and neighbors by planning a community career fair. You may choose to do the planning alone or with a group. You could invite organizations and businesses you have discovered and worked with to participate in the fair. They could provide information about their interests and services, give useful demonstrations, offer advice about problems, and provide printed materials that describe possible careers in detail.
In planning the fair, you'll want to:

■ Compile a list of all the organizations in your community that you would like to see represented.
■ Identify a contact at each organization whom you can call or write.
■ Select a place to hold the fair and set the date and time.
■ Identify all essential tasks and responsibilities and those individuals who will follow through on them.

After the fair, be sure to thank all participants and supporters who helped make it a success. (Follow program standards for troop money-earning projects in the GSUSA publication *Safety-Wise*.) Evaluate your fair. What went well? What could be improved?

Option 2: Plan a Trips and Speakers Project

Look at a career interest area in depth. Consider all the people who have careers in a particular area, as well as places where there are many jobs. Here are some suggestions for setting up your project.

Plan with a Group Discuss the career area in your community that you want to explore. Determine how much time you will give to this project and when you plan to carry it out.

Survey the Community   Make a list of possible trip sites and speakers. Consider including places where members of your family work. Use resources for trip ideas—business telephone directories, local business directories, newspapers.

Contact organizations and people in your community who can suggest interesting sites and speakers. You could contact business people's service organizations, local chapters of occupational interest groups, organizations committed to supporting the concerns and interests of women or minorities.

Develop a Detailed Plan   Discuss a choice of trips and speakers and the details of each trip/speaker—date, place, time. Divide and assign tasks and responsibilities.

Prepare for Each Trip/Speaker   Publicize each trip/speaker and complete all necessary arrangements.

Research the careers that will be discussed. You can prepare the career representative or speaker by giving her/him a list of your special interests, expectations, and questions.

Carry Out Your Plan   Follow safety standards throughout the activity (see the GSUSA publication *Safety-Wise*).

Follow Up   Write thank-you letters. Discuss your reactions and evaluate your project.

Option 3: Carry Out a Career Internship

A career internship gives you the opportunity to work with a career representative in a business or organization on a one-to-one basis. A career consultant is someone who has a career you are considering, and who will work with you intensively to help you understand the ins and outs of that career. You will have the chance to follow your consultant through typical workday activities, try out some of the tasks she/he does on the job, and learn about the general operations of the business or organization for which she/he works.

Contact your council, leader, or school personnel for names of people who could act as your career consultant. If you are interested in a consultant suggested by your council, determine with your council how to approach her/him. Plan ways with your consultant to individualize the career exploration experience to make it most appropriate for you.

If your council or leader does not know of a willing consultant who fits your career interest, don't let that stop you. Find your own consultant, checking with the council and your leader along the way. Here are some tips for selecting a consultant.

Identify Career Internship Possibilities   Make a list of the careers that interest you and the places where you could explore each career interest. Some sources for a potential consultants list are neighborhood stores; business telephone directories; your parents, neighbors, friends, teachers, guidance counselor; help wanted ads and regular advertising in the newspaper; community organizations and agencies; special interest clubs and organizations (women's groups, sports and recreation clubs, etc.).

Plan Your Approach   If you know of a person who you believe would be a good consultant, ask her/him right away. If not, list all consultants in order of choice. Then approach each one in turn. Decide on the best way to make your request. Wait for a final decision before going on to your next choice.

For a small business or organization, you could visit the manager when she/he is least likely to be busy and discuss your idea. For a large business, you could either write or call the personnel director to set up a convenient appointment to meet.

Contact a Potential Consultant Your appointment may be with a representative of the business or organization, or with a possible career consultant, or both.

The representative or career consultant you have selected may ask you questions about yourself, your interests, and why you are requesting a career internship. Be prepared to answer such questions.

Wait for an Answer Don't expect an answer to your request right away. After a week or so, call or visit your potential consultant to find out if she/he will work with you. Follow up until you get a firm yes or no decision.

Don't be disappointed if a potential business or consultant says no. She/he is not saying, "No, I don't want you." She/he is saying, "No, I am not able to be a part of a career internship at this time."

Whether the consultant says yes or no, you will want to thank her/him for considering your request. This follow-up call or visit will remind the potential consultant of your interest. Maybe she/he will be able to arrange an internship with a young woman sometime in the future, and the first person she/he thinks of might well be you.

Plan Your Career Internship Once a consultant says yes, you should start planning your experience together so that it fits both of your expectations.

Option 4: Get a Paying Job

Until now, you have probably explored career possibilities as a volunteer. Another rewarding way to learn about a career is through a paying job.

Many teenagers are eager to find jobs as soon as the labor laws of their state allow them to work. Parents may encourage young adults to work to help supplement the family income, to provide extra income for personal expenses, or to help pay for future expenses related to education, career training, or marriage.

Often, the jobs you have as a teenager do not fit your career goals perfectly. However, if you use the job-hunting resources that are available, you may be able to find a job that will advance your career plans. In any case, any paying job will be an important part of your personal and career development. It will help you to better understand the world of work and to decide how you can most effectively prepare for your chosen career direction.

Option 5: Start Your Own Business

Did you ever think of starting a business of your own? Many people find that owning a business gives them real independence and motivates them to work hard to increase their profits. If you decide to start your own business, there may be local clubs or organizations that can help you. You will learn many valuable skills, including how to meet community needs, how to plan a business venture, how to use your business profits, how to get along with fellow business people, and how to adhere to the laws regulating businesses in your community.

There are many businesses that a young woman can start. How many can you think of? Look in your local newspaper to determine the problems and needs of people in your community. Think about a business you could start to meet one or more of these needs.

Here, briefly, are the steps in starting a business:

I. Identify a need.

II. Determine how to fill the need through a service to be performed or the development of a product.

III. Plan and implement business operations:
A. Find out about laws that will affect you (insurance, liability, tax).
B. Set up facilities.
C. Make others aware of the availability of the service/product.
D. Obtain money to buy supplies.
E. Obtain supplies and materials.
F. Hire employees.
G. Plan production methods.
H. Set prices.
I. Produce the object (if a product-oriented business).
J. Advertise and market (sell) the service/product.
K. Implement accounting procedures; keep records.
L. Determine use of profits.

IV. Evaluate operations and improve where needed.

SENIOR GIRL SCOUT CHALLENGE

This Challenge asks you to put the Promise and Law into action. When you combine your talents and energies with your values and convictions, you can make a positive difference in the lives of others.

This Challenge has five sections. Each section has a preparation step (prep) followed by activities that challenge you to put what you have learned into action. Although you may do the sections in any order, it is recommended that you follow through in the order as numbered. You may work on these sections alone or with others who share your interests.

Section 1: Developing Your Potential

Prep   Read or reread the "Personal Development" and "Life Skills" chapters.

Complete the "me" interview and stress management activities on pages 21–22 and 68–69 of this handbook.

Challenge   Design your own self-development plan. Set some goals for yourself. Think about:

- What are some things that I want to do?
- What are my goals for the next year? five years? ten years?
- What do I want to start working on right now?
- What are my leisure and employment plans for the near future?

Follow through on your plan for a period of at least two months.

A goal might be to learn a skill, expand your ability to relate to others, practice budgeting, improve your figure, explore careers you are interested in, or anything that you feel will help you to develop your potential. Review the "Personal Development" chapter in this handbook to help you decide.

Section 2: Relating to Others

Prep Read or reread the "Relationships" chapter.

Complete three activities from this chapter that you have not already done, or design your own activity modeled after information presented in the chapter.

Challenge Examine your skills in relating to others. Plan to increase your skills in at least one area of relating.

Summarize your plan to increase your skills in relating to others: _____

_____

_____

_____

_____

Describe something you learned about yourself in doing the activities and completing your plan: _____

_____

_____

_____

_____

Section 3: Developing Values for Living

Prep Review the "Personal Development" chapter.

Complete all the activities in the "Values" section of that chapter (pages 24–25).

Challenge Decide on what you value the most. What issues or concerns carry great importance to you? Draw up a list of the ten things that you would most like to change and how. Put a star next to those items for which you can begin to make a change for the better right now. Decide how the Promise and Law can help you achieve positive change. Decide on at least three activities that you can and will do to make a positive change. If you work with others, be able to distinguish your own personal contributions to the effort.

Summarize your discoveries about yourself and your values.

What activities did you complete? Did you learn things about yourself after working on each one?

Think about this question: Did you find that what you actually say and do matches what you say you believe?

Section 4: Contributing to Society

Prep Read or reread the "Citizen of the World" chapter.

Challenge As a Girl Scout, you have probably been involved in many projects that contribute to your community's well-being. To complete this Challenge section, you must participate in a service project that will benefit your community in some way. You may join an effort directed by others or you may design, develop, and carry out your own effort. You may choose to work on this section alone or with others. Just be sure that you work on something you personally feel is important.

Your effort should total 15 hours. Review the "Citizen of the World" chapter for help in getting started. When you have completed the project, answer these questions.

1. Who benefited from this service project? How?
2. Which of my talents were best put to use?
3. What skills and abilities would I like to develop further?
4. What did I learn about myself and my values?

Section 5: Helping Others Know About Girl Scouting

Prep Review the "About Girl Scouting" and "Wider Opportunities" chapters of this handbook. If possible, read the Girl Scout information sections of a leaders' guide to a Girl Scout handbook.

Challenge Get involved in Girl Scouting beyond your troop. You may select an activity from the ones listed or develop your own plan to help others know about Girl Scouting.

- Serve on a councilwide girl planning group.
- Help plan a Cadette or Senior Girl Scout conference, Thinking Day event, or other special event.
- Serve on the council board or one of the committees or task groups in your council.
- Participate in a council-sponsored training conference or event involving Girl Scout volunteers.
- Plan and carry out a project that will explain the origin, purpose, and use of the Juliette Low World Friendship Fund.
- Conduct tours of council properties/facilities.
- Provide home hospitality for Girl Guides or Girl Scouts from other countries or other parts of this country.
- Participate in activities sponsored by Campus Girl Scouts.

After you have completed your total Challenge, all five sections, use the evaluation guide below to help you and your leader evaluate your experience.

- What have I discovered about the world of Girl Scouting?
- In what situations have I demonstrated a real understanding of the Promise and Law by applying them to everyday living?
- How has my project benefited others?
- What are some possible ways that I could continue to show my concern in this area in the future?
- In what ways have I shown that I am capable of self-direction? In what ways am I able to work, plan, and share with a group?
- What other things have I learned about myself?
- How have I demonstrated what I value?

GIRL SCOUT GOLD AWARD

The Girl Scout Gold Award is the highest achievement in Girl Scouting. Your efforts to earn this award express a special commitment to yourself, your community, your world, and the future. This award has five requirements;

requirements 1–4 may be done in any order but they must be completed before you work on the fifth requirement, the Girl Scout Gold Award project.

Requirements (requirements started prior to Senior Girl Scouting may not be applied toward this award):

1. Earn four interest project patches.
2. Earn the Career Exploration pin.
3. Earn the Senior Girl Scout Leadership Award.
4. Earn the Senior Girl Scout Challenge.
5. Do a Girl Scout Gold Award project.

A Girl Scout Gold Award project is an extension and a combination of all that you have learned in your previous Girl Scout work. The first four requirements helped you develop skills, practice leadership, explore career possibilities, and discover more about yourself. All of this will be put into action when you design and carry out this special project. Your project may be done with others, but with each step, it will be important to think about the special contributions you bring to the work and to realize that you are working on something that you personally feel is important.

Complete the project steps in order.

Step 1   Identify your personal talents and strengths that can be put into action through a Girl Scout Gold Award project.

Step 2   Decide on an area that you care about and in which you would like to do something to demonstrate your commitment to yourself, your community, and the future. Develop an action plan that will require your commitment and effort over a period of at least four months. Write your plan on the form shown on pages 165–166.

Step 3   Identify the people with whom you will be working. Be sure to include your leader, adviser, and/or adult partners.

Step 4   Send your plan to your Girl Scout council office. Your leader or adult adviser should work with you on completing the project plan notice. This plan must be sent to your council office at least six weeks prior to putting your plan into action. This provides your council with an opportunity to support you in your efforts, enhance your project, and prepare for honoring your accomplishments. Both you and your council should agree that the plan for your Girl Scout Gold Award project is acceptable.

Step 5   Your council will respond to your plan within this six-week period and will let you know whether your plan is acceptable. If your council has recommendations for change, they will contact you. Together you can agree on revisions.

If you have not received notice within three weeks that your council has received your plan, a follow-up call or letter is advisable. You should also keep a copy of your plan. You and/or your leader should make sure that you have received acknowledgment to proceed before you begin your project.

Be sure to stick to the plan. If there are major changes, you should contact your council. Remember that your work should extend over a period of at least four months.

Upon completion of the project, write a brief project report in the format shown on pages 167–168. Send the report to your council office or other designated address as notification that you have completed your Girl Scout Gold Award work.

For more information and sample exemplary projects, please refer to the *Girl Scout Gold Award Booklet*.

APPRENTICE TRAINER'S PIN

Senior Girl Scouts with leadership experience can qualify as candidates for the Apprentice Trainer's pin (Level 1). To qualify as an apprentice trainer you must:

- Have completed an LIT project
- Be at least 15 years of age or entering tenth grade
- Have completed a train-the-trainer course

As an apprentice trainer applicant, you should meet the director of training for your council (or someone she has designated) to determine your readiness to take on this leadership role. Once you have been appointed as an apprentice trainer, you will conduct courses for girls (for example, a leadership course for LITs or CITs), leaders, and other adult volunteers. Together with your council director of training (or designate), you will agree to teach a specific number of courses. For at least half of these courses, you will work with an experienced or master trainer who has taken special training and has already served as an apprentice trainer for at least one year.

TEN-YEAR AWARD

Girls who have been members of Girl Scouting for ten years prior to becoming 18 years of age or completing senior high school are entitled to receive the Ten-Year Award. These years do not have to have been continuous.

BRIDGE TO ADULT GIRL SCOUTS PIN

Senior Girl Scouts who are 17 years of age or in the final year of high school are ready to embark on their life's career. As an adult, a young woman will most likely find that her life's career includes many diverse experiences and is shaped and changed by personal and professional experiences. Your future may include college, technical training, employment, hobbies, other interests.

One thing that your future can include is continued commitment to Girl Scouting. You may have already had many experiences that helped you learn about the roles adults play in Girl Scouting. Earning the Bridge to Adult Girl Scouts pin will broaden your knowledge and enable you to continue your commitment to Girl Scouting. Each step describes a general activity. It will be up to you to design a specific activity for completing the step. Although it is recommended that you do the steps in order, it is acceptable to change the sequence as opportunities arise. You will be entitled to receive the Bridge to Adult Girl Scouts pin when you have completed the eight bridging steps described below.

1. Find out how Girl Scouting is organized in your community.
2. Find out about the roles adults fill in Girl Scouting.
3. Work with a Girl Scout adult.
4. Help others learn about the benefits of Girl Scouting.
5. Find out about the training and learning experiences available to adults in Girl Scouting. If possible, participate in one of these.
6. Take on a leadership role in Girl Scouting. This could be as an LIT, a CIT, an apprentice trainer, or through a special internship available in your council.
7. Plan a bridging ceremony.
8. Plan and do a summer Girl Scout activity.

Recognitions that can be earned by both Senior and Cadette Girl Scouts are described under "Recognitions for Cadette and Senior Girl Scouts," pages 149–152.

Campus Girl Scouts

Young adults who are attending colleges, universities, junior colleges, vocational or technical schools, or other institutions of higher learning may belong to Campus Girl Scout groups. These groups may be coeducational, since membership as an adult in Girl Scouting is open to men as well as to women. Campus Girl Scout groups may focus on the three C's—council, campus, and community. Ultimately, the groups work on behalf of girl members through the support they give to the Girl Scout council that sponsors them. Some of the activities that Campus Girl Scouts participate in are:

- Helping on campus with freshman orientation
- Assisting Girl Scout leaders in taking trips, tours, hikes, etc.
- Serving as program consultants
- Conducting college tours and providing live-in campus experiences for Senior Girl Scouts
- Assisting with senior citizen projects
- Planning events with other Campus Girl Scout groups

Campus Girl Scouts are entitled to wear a special CGS guard with the membership pin.

Mix and Match—Girl Scouting Fits Everywhere

"I'm too busy with classes and extracurricular activities at school. I just don't have enough time to really get involved with Girl Scout recognitions."

Schoolwork, dating, after-school sports are just a few of the potential demands on your time. But, Girl Scouting can be a part of all of this.

See page 3 for ideas on how to mix and match Girl Scouting with all the other things in your life. Consolidate your efforts. Girl Scouting can be a part of all that you do, and all your interests can become a part of your Girl Scout experience. You chart the course for all the fun and learning that is possible.

Girl Scout Silver Award Report Form

Requirements 1–4 must be completed prior to beginning requirement 5.

1. Interest Project Patches
Titles: **Date Completed**   **Leader/Consultant Signature**

_____   _____   _____

_____   _____   _____

_____   _____   _____

2. Career Exploration
(check one)   **Date Completed**   **Leader/Consultant Signature**

___ From Dreams to Reality activities patch

___ Career Exploration interest project   _____   _____

patch

3. Leadership
(check one)   **Date Completed**   **Leader/Consultant Signature**

___ Cadette Girl Scout Leadership Award

___ Leadership interest project patch   _____   _____

4. Cadette Girl Scout Challenge   **Date Completed**   **Leader/Consultant Signature**

                                                 _____   _____

5. Girl Scout Silver Award Project
A. List the skills, talents, and abilities that you put into action.

_____

_____

_____

_____

_____

B. Briefly describe (three to six sentences) your plan and your reasons for selecting this project.

_____

_____

_____

_____

_____

(OVER)

C. List those people who worked with you on your project.

_____   _____

_____   _____

_____   _____

_____   _____

_____   _____

D. Briefly evaluate (three to six sentences) your completed project.

_____

_____

_____

_____

_____

_____

_____

_____

_____

_____

_____

_____

_____

Leader/Consultant Signature

_____

Your Signature

_____

Date Completed

Girl Scout Gold Award Project Plan

Submit this project plan to your council office prior to carrying out
your Girl Scout Gold Award project.

**1. Interest Project Patches
Titles:**   **Date Completed**   **Leader/Consultant Signature**

_____   _____   _____

_____   _____   _____

_____   _____   _____

_____   _____   _____

_____   _____   _____

**2. Career Exploration Pin
Option Completed:**   **Date Completed**   **Leader/Consultant Signature**

                                             _____   _____

**3. Senior Girl Scout Leadership Award
Activities:**   **Date Completed**   **Leader/Consultant Signature**

_____   _____   _____

_____   _____   _____

_____   _____   _____

_____   _____   _____

**4. Senior Girl Scout
Challenge**   **Date Completed**   **Leader/Consultant Signature**

                                             _____   _____

5. Girl Scout Gold Award Project Plan
A. Describe your strengths, talents, and skills that will be put into action.

_____

_____

_____

_____

_____

_____

(OVER)

B. Briefly describe (three to six sentences) what you plan to do for your Girl Scout Gold Award project.

_____

_____

_____

_____

_____

Describe why you have selected this project.

_____

_____

_____

_____

List the consultants and resources that will help you complete your project.

_____   _____

_____   _____

_____   _____

_____   _____

What do you hope to accomplish with your project? Who will benefit?

_____

_____

_____

_____

_____

_____   _____
Date   Your Signature

                                _____
                                Your Address

Girl Scout Gold Award Project Report Form

1. Write a brief description of your project (three or four sentences).

_____

_____

_____

_____

_____

2. Describe the personal strengths, talents, and skills utilized in the project.

_____

_____

_____

_____

_____

3. How did your project benefit others?

_____

_____

_____

_____

_____

4. What did you learn about yourself as a result of this project?

_____

_____

_____

_____

_____

_____

(OVER)

5. What aspects of your project would you change or do differently?

_____

_____

_____

_____

_____

_____

_____

6. What was the most successful aspect of your project?

_____

_____

_____

_____

_____

_____

_____

_____

Leader/Consultant Signature(s)

_____

_____

_____   _____
Your Address   Your Signature

                                       _____
                                       Date Completed

INDEX